The Omnipotent Child

The Omnipotent Child

How To Mold, Strengthen and Perfect the Developing Child

Thomas P Millar, MD

Third Edition
1994

The Omnipotent Child
How to Mold, Strengthen and Perfect the Developing Child

© Thomas P. Millar 1983, 1989,1994

Canadian Catalogue in Publishing Data
Millar, Thomas P. (Thomas Palmer) 1923
The Omnipotent child

Includes bibliographical references and index.
ISBN 0-9693271-7-X

1. Child rearing. 2. Problem children I. Title
HQ773.M54 1994   649'153   C94- 910133-8

Published by
TDL Enterprises Ltd.
Palmer Press Division
1380 Maple Street
Vancouver, B.C.
V6J 3R9

Printed in Canada by FriesenPrinters

International Standard Book Number 0 - 9693271 - 7 - X

CONTENTS

Preface to the Third Edition

Webster defines discipline as training which moulds, strengthens and perfects. The aspect of child rearing most difficult to manage is this training. It is as important as loving the child for it leads him to patience and self control, consideration for others, and appropriate respect for the rules of society. It is the widespread lack of such training that has led to violence in children and youth, much learning failure and widespread social incompetence.

There is a pattern to children who have been poorly trained. They are impulsive and impatient, egocentric and socially inept, determined to make their own rules and, despite their arrogance they have poor self esteem. I described this pattern in 1983 when the first edition of *The Omnipotent Child* was published. At that time I was dealing exclusively with pre-adolescent children and the parenting programs I designed were addressed to their specific problems. I began to call this remedial parenting.

However, my book changed my practice. Since I had traced the origins of the omnipotent child syndrome back to adaptive training in the pre-school years, parents began bringing their pre-school children to me. In the last decade over sixty percent of my practice has been thus. I have begun to think of myself as a child-rearing consultant.

In 1989 I rewrote The Omnipotent Child adding a chapter which I called a Little Preventing Parenting. Since then I have come to realize, I have been trying to kill two birds with the same stone. Mothers of pre-school children read the part of the book relevant to their problems, and mothers of pre-adolescent children for whom prevention was no longer the name of the game, skipped the chapter. A partial waste of time for both parties.

Clearly two books were needed. This is the first of those books. I am now preparing another addressed to mothers of pre-school children

The Omnipotent Child III, is an abridged, and rewritten, version of the Omnipotent Child II. It is intended for parents whose elmentary age children are having some growing up difficulties. It is intended to help these parents bring their child out of his difficulties.

Previous editions of *The Omnipotent Child* have been criticized for the space taken up with sociological and philosophical issues concerning the state of the family . Since I have had my say, I have removed much of this material. But I could not resist a short appendix entitled Son of Big Chilly. I have also added a much needed Appendix which deals with Attention Deficit Disorder.

The only thing I feel my readers will want to locate through an Index is one or another of my management programs. To my surprise I discovered there were no less than fifteen of these. So, if you want to check back on my Getting Dressed Program, or going to Bed on Time, or how to handle Stealing, look it up in the Index.

T.P.Millar, Vancouver, B.C. 1994

1

The Dewey Syndrome

An unusual child has been growing up in America in recent times, a child so different from what his parents are, or wished him to be, that sometimes they wonder how they could have produced him. For forty years it has been my privilege to sit in the eye of this particular hurricane. I have observed how many parents set about rearing their children. I have spent many hours in my playroom encountering these children in all their provocative glory.

As the years passed I began to perceive a pattern in the children and saw that this outcome was usually associated with specific difficulties in parenting. For reasons that will become clear as we proceed, I elected to call this pattern the Omnipotent Child Syndrome. Let me begin by drawing a picture of a family in such difficulty.

Dewey is nine years old and in the fourth grade at Brookside School. His teacher, Miss Grant, called Dewey's mother one day in early December.

"He never finishes his seat work," Miss Grant said. "He starts, but the first little stumbling block he encounters, a number fact he can't remember or an unfamiliar reading word, and he grinds to a halt, looks at the wall as though he hopes to find the answer blazoned there. Then off he goes daydreaming. Then first thing you know he's whispering, or throwing spitballs. Lately it seems a day doesn't pass that he doesn't disrupt the class."

"I had no idea," Mother declared. After all this was December and the first time Miss Grant had called.

"I don't like to alarm the parents unnecessarily," Miss Grant said. "But I can't stand over him all day, you know. I mean he is in fourth grade. He should be able to do a little seat work without constant supervision. I do have other children, you know. Some of them a good deal less bright than Dewey."

"Oh! I understand, Miss Grant," Mother said. "And I really do appreciate the extra effort you've taken." As it happens Mother had been hoping things would be better this year, and as time passed with no word from the school, she had allowed herself to believe that they were. Her disappointment was acute.

"I don't mind individualizing my approach," Miss Grant said. "And I have. But things have not improved one iota. He's still not finishing half the assignments."

"Perhaps if you kept him after school," Mother offered, not really thinking this will work, but responding to the fact that Miss Grant seemed to expect her to suggest something.

"Oh, I have," Miss Grant said grimly, "but that doesn't do any good either. Unless I stand right over him, he just sits there till the time's up. We are only allowed to keep them half an hour, you know."

Mother nodded. He's the same at home when it comes to taking out the garbage or cleaning his room. Unless she stands right over him nothing gets done.

"He doesn't seem to feel any obligation to do the school work," Miss Grant said. "Lots of children his age worry if an assignment's late, but not him. I don't think he cares."

Miss Grant, remembering the incident that made her decide to call, went on. "Today, I told him I was not going to let him get away without finishing his math assignment. He gave me **that** look! So I told him, 'Dewey, if you haven't finished that page of math by recess, I'm keeping you in, but if I have to, you're going to be sorry.'"

"He didn't finish it?"

"He did nothing. Deliberately! So I kept him in." Miss Grant paused a moment. "If looks could kill I'd have been dead a million times over. That's when I told him."

"Told him?"

"'Dewey,'" I said, 'Life has obligations and life has privileges. If you don't meet your obligations, you don't get your privileges.'" Miss Grant paused. Mother murmured the expected agreement. Miss Grant continued. "'Since you did not meet your obligation, then you are going to lose a privilege.'" Miss Grant paused again.

"Of course," Mother agreed. Even so, she was sure that kind of talk wouldn't impress Dewey.

"You know what he did then?" Miss Grant asked. "He yawned. Right in my face."

"Oh dear!" Mother said. "Perhaps he was just tired and didn't mean to be rude?"

"Rude! In a moment you'll hear rude." Miss Grant picked up the thread of her story. "So I said to him, 'Dewey, it's your job to do all your assignments. And on time. You didn't do your math so you are not going on tomorrow's field trip with the rest of the class.'"

Mother flinched.

Miss Grant continued. "'But it's dumb math,' Dewey said. So I told him, 'Dewey, the math isn't dumb. What you mean is you don't like doing it. But you still have to do it. There are other kids who don't like the math, but they do it. Life's like that; sometimes we have to do things we don't like. Sometimes, when you do a thing you don't like, you start getting interested in it. The first thing you know it's your favorite subject.'"

"He didn't buy it?" Mother asked, knowing the answer.

"He did not!" Miss Grant paused while she transferred the telephone to her other ear. "What he said was, 'OK! OK! I'll do the dumb math. Tomorrow, when we get back from the field trip.'" Miss Grant snorted. "No way. Once we were back from the trip fat chance I'd have of getting any work out of him. 'No Dewey,' I said, 'You can work while we are on the field trip, because you are not going.'"

Now, Mother told herself, comes the rude bit.

"You should have heard him. I mean whatever came into his mind came out of his mouth. 'You can't keep me from going on that field trip. You're not the boss of me. I don't have to do what you say. Kids got rights.' He pulled out all the stops." Miss Grant, who had waxed progressively more indignant, snapped. "He ended by calling me a bossy old bitch, and gave me the Nazi salute. I don't have to take that kind of thing, you know."

Mother tried to apologize , but Miss Grant was not in a mood to listen to apologies.

"I yelled at him, I admit it. And I don't believe in yelling at children, but Migawd, it would take a saint." Miss Grant paused a moment. "You have to understand I had a class of children watching this performance. I couldn't let him get away with that kind of thing and retain control of my class from then on." Miss Grant barely stopped for breath. "Not that he's got a friend in the class, he's so bossy. Every recess you can hear him out on the playground giving everybody orders."

Stung by the vivid picture Miss Grant was painting, Mother said, "I wish you'd called me earlier in the year. Dewey's father and I don't believe he ought to act like that."

"I just wanted you to know," Miss Grant said, "that he'll be coming home, and God knows what his version will be."

"Thank you for alerting me," Mother replied.

"He spent the day in the principal's office," Miss Grant said. "His last words to me were not to expect him to come to my dumb old school again." Miss Grant laughed weakly. "I wouldn't be too surprised if he had a stomach ache tomorrow."

And he did.

Often, it isn't until some such crisis in the school or community erupts that parents realize their child isn't just going through a difficult phase which he will outgrow. Chances are friends and maybe even the doctor have endorsed this view on occasion, but it isn't easy facing up to the realization that one's child is not making it. It suggests, does it not, that the parenting hasn't quite done the job it is supposed to do?

Unless you can find another explanation that exonerates!

There are a lot of ways not to face up such as blaming the other kids, or the teacher, or sugar, or some mysterious cerebral condition without neurological findings that is interfering with his ability to concentrate.(See Appendix A) Many a parent has struggled with a such notions for a while before they found their way to my consulting room.

When they do, my first task is to assemble a picture of this family and their Dewey by obtaining a history from the parents, interviewing the child, and finally, as the situation warrants, contacting other persons with knowledge of the problem, usually the teacher, if she is willing to talk to me. Sometimes I need to arrange for special examinations such as psychological or neurological tests.

Let me now take you, step by step, through such a diagnostic sequence. Since it is the most important of the steps, let's start with the history.

History

It is my practice to ask both parents to attend the initial visit. Although the mother could probably give an accurate history on her own, it is helpful to have the father there, not only because one gets a chance to observe the relationship of the parents to one another, but also because doing so involves both parents in seeking the solution to the problem.

Mothers usually begin giving the history. Fathers, not too sure they approve of the whole enterprise, tend to hang back. In general women are less threatened asking for help than men are. However, if the advice given does not conform to the woman's prejudgments about the situation, she is much more liable to dismiss it out of hand than is a man.

So Dewey's mother, Lydia, nervously mangling her gloves but putting on a brave front, told me about the school crisis, and passed from this to an account of her own concerns about Dewey.

"He dawdles getting dressed in the morning. It's just like Miss Grant says, he doesn't do anything unless you're standing right there, keeping him moving. He'd never do his teeth if I didn't supervise." Mother moved back from the edge of her chair. "As for cleaning his room, forget it."

"He simply refuses to do things?" I asked.

"He doesn't actually refuse. Most of the time it's 'inna minute, Ma.' But his minutes tend to stretch."

"And stretch," Frank, the father, muttered.

"It takes at least two reminders to get him started dressing. Or anything else for that matter," Lydia continued.

"Six tellings and a yelling," Frank corrected.

Mother defended a little. "Eventually he starts, but he soon grinds to a halt. Five minutes later I find him day dreaming at the window or making faces at himself in the mirror."

"Going to bed's the same," Frank said. "Until you threaten him he doesn't think you mean business."

"But we shouldn't have to threaten him to get him to do things, should we?" Lydia asked.

Recognizing a loaded question when I hear one, I glanced over at the father.

"Threatening is no worse than nagging," Frank said.

They both looked at me.

"I gather you've both tried hard to get him to meet his responsibilities, but nothing seems to work?" I countered.

Lydia nodded a vehement agreement. "It's his job to take out the garbage. I remind him. He always says he's going to, after the next commercial, but he always forgets."

"You should just turn off the TV," Frank said. "And don't turn it back on until he has finished the job."

"I've tried that," Lydia complained. "We always end up in a battle-of-wills. 'I'm not taking out the garbage until you turn that TV back on.' 'I'm not turning that TV back on until you take out that garbage.'" Lydia shrugged helplessly.

"And it's never Dewey who weakens first," Frank observed.

"Frank thinks I'm too easy on Dewey."

"Well! Aren't you?" Frank countered.

"If I am," Lydia replied, smiling with her teeth, "It's to make up for your strictness, dear!"

"Oh no!" Frank protested. "You've got it backwards. If I'm strict, it's to make up for your being too easy."

"If you were home with him all day," Lydia said. "You'd find yourself giving in too." She sighed. "Sometimes it's easier to do it yourself than yell at him."

"It certainly sounds as if Dewey hasn't much patience when it comes to doing things he doesn't enjoy." I interjected, addressing my remark to Frank. I could see Lydia is getting upset and, to avoid them traumatizing each other too badly at this juncture, I chose to give her a rest.

Frank, opting to participate, nodded in agreement. "He has no patience at all. If he can't get out of some duty, he does the absolute minimum. "

Mother nodded and looked miserably into her lap.

"Another thing," Frank continued. "Everything has to be now. He can't wait for dessert. If he's playing a game he can't wait for his turn. And if he's losing you can be sure we're all going to be accused of cheating. Or he'll quit playing."

Frank's directness was making Lydia uncomfortable and though Frank knew it, he continued anyway.

"Just two nights ago, I left him doing a page of math. I came back later to check. Such a mess, numbers not in columns, crossing out, half-erased scribbles. More than half the answers were wrong. I ended up wondering if he hadn't started putting down any number at all, just to make it look as if he had done the work."

"Math isn't his favorite subject," Lydia offered nervously.

"Work isn't his favorite subject," Frank snapped. "If it isn't fun, Dewey doesn't think it's fair to put it on him."

"Apparently he hasn't developed much tolerance for tedium" I intervened. "How does he handle other unpleasures? Say some disappointment? Supposing some pleasure he had been counting on didn't work out, how does he handle that?"

Frank shook his head. "Although he's nine, he's liable to cry like a three year old."

"Now Frank," Lydia protested. "Be fair."

What she means is be loyal. It is a real problem for parents to report their children's symptoms. It seems disloyal to do so. Many have to preface each complaint with some extenuating remark such as 'All kids are like that,' or 'He can be very well behaved when he wants to.'

At this moment, Frank was not feeling a need to extenuate. "I am being fair," he said, not about to have his serve broken. "In fact, just the other night I took him and his friend Kenny to a movie. When we got there, there was a big line. I could see we weren't going to make it when the picture changed so I suggested we go to the corner for a milkshake and then home. No way! He insisted on waiting. Well, we didn't get in, and guess who started crying." Frank shook his head. "Right there in front of the theater."

"He'd been looking forward to that movie for a whole week," Lydia said in extenuation.

"On the way home," Frank continued, "he got really mad, and I mean mad. He wanted to sue the theater owner for false advertising or child abuse, anything to get even. The least he was going to settle for was a letter to the editor. I wouldn't be surprised if he writes one; He's like that. If anybody crosses him, look out."

"Oh Frank!" Lydia exclaimed as she administered the coup de grâce to her mangled gloves.

"But Lydia, you know he's like that."

"If he is," Lydia said, close to tears, "we did it to him."

If he is, we did it to him.

There, expressed in a phrase, stands one of the most serious impediments to child rearing extant these days: the notion that, whatever the child is, the parent did to him. It's as though the child brought nothing to the relationship at all, as though all children were equally easy to rear, and if this one isn't doing well it must be the parents' fault.

What we are dealing with here is guilt, naked and unadorned. There is a strong pull on the psychiatrist to respond to this with some reassurance, but it would be premature to do so at this time.

Often a simple, "Why don't we leave deciding how you've got where you are with Dewey until we have the whole picture and can give some thought to what we can do about it," is sufficient to keep the history taking from bogging down in a morass of mea culpas and mutual blaming.

It is often wise, when tensions are high like this, to move the discussion into some less loaded area, perhaps to earlier times when mothering was more joyful and the things to be reported about Dewey less critical. So I asked Lydia, "Tell me, what was he like as a baby?"

Dewey turned out to have been an amiable, responsive infant, lively but not overactive, fairly intense in his reactive style, quite easily distracted, certainly not one of your can-entertain- himself-for-hours babies. However he was regular, the product of a normal pregnancy and an uneventful birth. It is clear, he may have been a bit challenging to rear, especially for a first-time mother, but there is nothing really pathological or even far out about his temperament.

Of course, children's temperaments vary, which makes some of them harder to rear than others, especially for some mothers. And there is such a thing as a temperamental match. If some sweet southern lady, raised in the gentle tradition, and unlikely to say damn if a hammer fell on her toe, has a placid, sunny and accommodating little girl, things are liable to go swimmingly. But give her a high energy, intense, moody boy, and tensions may mount. Then, because she is as civilized as she is, the madder Mother gets the more protective she becomes, and soon the child- rearing fat is in the ambivalent fire.

Since temperamental characteristics are inherited, reasonable parent-child matches tend to occur quite often. With adopted children, of course, such inherited matching cannot occur, which may be an important reason so many adopted children seem to get into psychological growing-up difficulties.

In any case, it is important to try to get a picture of what the child brings to the parent-child interaction, to determine what kind of a baby this particular mother was given to rear. The temperamental characteristics that complicate things mostly involve high energy level, distractibility, and intensity. If you have to put your knee on his chest to change his diaper, prepare yourself for a stormy parenthood.

ask Mom

Also of great relevance is the mother's circumstances when she began parenting. Depression, financial worries, or health problems can all complicate the task.

Dewey's mother was surprised to find herself pregnant and, like most women in that situation, soon became enthusiastic about the enterprise. Neither parent had any serious health, family or personal problems to complicate things in these last few years. Dewey's father changed his job not long after the baby was born, but there were no serious problems. Like most young people they didn't have money to waste, but neither have they had serious financial worries to absorb their energies.

In fact things had gone swimmingly until Dewey was two years old. "I just never believed the terrible twos could be that terrible," Lydia said. "Suddenly he was so cranky and demanding. Wouldn't let me out of his sight. He seemed to expect me to entertain him all day long."

"If he said jump," Frank interjected, "we were supposed to come to attention, salute, and ask, 'how high dear?' Which one of us did more than was good for him, or her."

"One of us!" Lydia said, rolling her eyes.

"Dewey sounds as though he still expects that response," I commented.

"He may not issue orders as bluntly as he used to," Frank said, "but no way will he accept that we have a right to set limits on him."

"Everything turns into a battle-of-wills," Lydia said. "I don't know how to avoid it. I try to be fair." Lydia shook her head. "Sometimes I get the feeling he wants to argue, that he's looking for something to argue about."

"Make a good lawyer," Frank muttered.

If all of the children parents have told me would make good lawyers had become such, the world would be swamped with lawyers. Come to think of it, it is!

"We tell him bedtime in ten minutes," Lydia said. "He pleads, 'just until this show is over.' Well, if that's maybe fifteen minutes, I say 'OK, but get in your pajamas during the commercial.'"

"Which he doesn't," Frank said.

"Even though he promised," Lydia agreed. "And then he gives me an argument: 'Why do I have to go to bed, you're staying up.' I try to tell him that's because we're the adults."

"He doesn't buy it," Frank said. "He thinks he should have all the prerogatives of an adult."

"Do you make him go to bed then?"

"Oh yes. He doesn't get to stay up. Well, I mean not as late as us." She shook her head. "Sometimes, I get tired of arguing, and let him have one more show. I know it's wrong, but after a day of Dewey, it's hard to stay firm."

"Do you ever punish him for not getting to bed on time?"

"Oh, punishment never does any good. If you take away some TV he just says he wasn't going to watch anyway. You can't punish him, because nothing bothers him."

"He always finds something else to do," Frank agreed. "And makes damn sure we know he isn't suffering."

"I don't like to punish," Lydia said. "I don't think child rearing should be parents ordering and kids obeying. It should be *a democratic relationship of equals,* shouldn't it?"

I know the book she's checking me out on, but I'm not about to let the history-taking deteriorate into a philosophical discussion on parenting. However, before I had to field the question, Frank jumped in.

"Dewey would never settle for just being equal. He wants to be in charge. His idea of fair is what suits Dewey. He has no idea that fair for him might be unfair for somebody else."

"He's a bit self-centred at times," Lydia acknowledged. "But then he's only nine years old."

"A little self-centered! You ought to hear him playing in the yard," Frank said. "He's Attila the Hun, organizing the troops. No wonder they go home."

Lydia sighed. "It's getting so he plays with younger children a lot of the time."

"They'll do what he tells them to," Frank explained.

"These battles-of-wills," I asked, "are they over important things?"

"No! Usually some little thing," Lydia replied. "But once he gets his back up, he's got to win. Even if it means settling for one tiny concession, 'just three minutes more, Mom.'"

"That's winning," Frank said. "That's what's really going on. Winning! Only three more minutes maybe, but then he won."

"Three more minutes doesn't hurt," Lydia muttered.

"Not getting it sure hurts him," Frank argued.

"It sounds as though that little concession has become a matter of pride to him."

"Exactly," Frank said. "If he goes to bed when we say, he acknowledges our authority. To him that's a put down, and no way will he accept that."

"We aren't trying to put him down," Lydia said. "He just sees everything that way. It hurts his self- esteem."

"Other kids go to bed when they are told, and it doesn't seem to hurt their self-esteem," Frank objected.

There was a pause. They seemed a little spent having covered so much painful ground.

"Then you think his self-esteem is not too good?" I asked Lydia.

"Oh yes."

"He may sound arrogant," Frank agreed. "But he really isn't that sure about himself. It shows."

Lydia nodded. "Sometimes he says it right out. 'I'm dumb. Nobody likes me. I can't do anything right.'"

"But he's not dumb," Frank said. "Already he reads *Time*." He grinned. "If that counts. And he understands numbers, even if it's like pulling teeth to get him to do times tables."

"And he has to be perfect," Lydia added. "He can't lose a game. He can't accept that his father and I can bowl better than he. He seems to feel that if he doesn't come first, he's no good at all. He never seems to make allowances for himself as a child."

later on

"He doesn't think he is," Frank explained. "He expects a full voice in adult affairs. And often gets it. Somehow or other we always end up doing things his way."

"Not always, Frank."

"Well, maybe not always," Frank conceded. "But who chooses the restaurant when we go out for dinner?"

"Frank, you like Chinese," Lydia protested.

"That's not the point. I also like Italian."

"And Armenian. And Mexican, and . . ." Lydia smiled. It was the first time she had done so since the session began.

"I'll tell you one area in which Dewey reigns supreme," Frank said. "Vacations. No way are we allowed to go on vacations without him."

"You haven't been away from him at all?"

"Not since he was four, and your mother came for two weeks," Frank said.

"But we do go out in the evenings."

"To a chorus of 'Where are you going? When will you be back? Why can't I go? Will you call me when you get there? Be sure and leave the number so I can reach you if I need to'," Frank said.

"Sounds like he has a little trouble with separation," I commented.

"Sometimes," Lydia acknowledged.

"At night?" I ask.

"Wants someone to lie down with him. He'd come into our bed if I didn't draw the line. I think he is a little too attached to his mother."

"He's just a child, Frank."

"He worries when you're not there?" I asked Lydia.

"A little."

"Lydia! If you're ten minutes late getting home from somewhere he's checking out the window every two minutes. And he's always after you to quit smoking." Frank turned to me. "Doesn't want her to get cancer."

I can see Dewey's concern pleases his mother a little. I haven't the heart to tell her that what he is probably worried about is not her, but who will look after him, if she isn't around. Not that he will admit he needs looking after, of course!

"Then you and Frank haven't really been away from Dewey for . . . almost six years I guess?"

"Has it really been that long?" Frank asked the wall.

"Don't forget, we went to Seattle that weekend," Lydia said.

Frank reached over and placed his hand on hers. "And you spent the whole weekend wondering whether Dewey was surviving."

"Not the whole weekend."

Gradually I pieced together a picture of Dewey's style. He is an avoider. If he is to participate in some new activity like Little League or swimming lessons, he's all gung-ho until the time nears, then he's not so sure, and it takes quite a bit of encouragement to get him there. He's OK for a time or two, but soon it's "Aw, baseball is dumb."

"He expects to be Mickey Mantle first time out," Frank said, "and when that doesn't happen, he loses interest."

I discovered that Dewey hasn't many friends. He tends to run through friendships quickly, alienating the kids with his bossiness and insistence that things focus around him. Now he plays with younger children, and one boy who's a lot like him.

"I guess they have to settle for each other," Frank said.

While Dewey talks big, he is really quite timid. He's beginning to isolate himself, to spend more time watching TV rather than playing outside. His favorites are the cartoon super heroes. Sometimes, when his father isn't around, he talks about earrings and dying his hair green.

Despite all these negatives, Dewey has no major symptoms. He may want to avoid school a bit, but it doesn't amount to a real phobia. He's difficult, but he isn't really malicious or destructive. Despite his poor work habits, he's learning what he needs to know, and I'm sure he's up to grade level in achievement. He has no habit disorders, doesn't wet or soil, doesn't steal, and while he sometimes shades the truth in his favor a bit, he isn't a blatant liar.

"He isn't a bad kid," Frank said. "But if he doesn't get over some of these ways soon, he's going to have real problems when he's older."

"How do you think he's going to feel about coming in to see me?" I asked them. Many parents worry about this, and Dewey's are no exception. I like to tell them how to manage things.

"No matter how you present it, chances are he's going to be negative about coming, but don't worry about that. Most kids are pretty uncertain about this kind of situation. My concern is that he doesn't arrive at my office under the impression he's going to get his eyes checked."

They smile. They can see how that might lead to trouble.

"It's best to select one unequivocal symptom," I tell them, "one he cannot possibly deny, and focus on that."

Since they seemed uncertain I spelled it out for them. "Present it to him like this," I said. "'Dewey, we get crosswise, you and I. It happens like this. I want you to do something you don't want to do. The first thing you know we're yelling at each other. You don't like it, and I don't like it, but it keeps happening. We don't seem to be able to find our way out of it. Dr. Millar is a doctor for that kind of problem. We've been to see him and told him about our family. Now he wants to meet you and see what kind of a boy you are.'"

"I can just hear him," Frank interjected. "'I'm not crazy, I'm not going to any shrink.'"

"Frank!" Lydia said.

"Sorry!" Frank said.

"If being called a shrink upsets a man, he oughtn't to be in child psychiatry." I laughed. "I get worse you know. Just the other day one of my office kids, a little annoyed that I was slipping his mother out from under his thumb, said to me, 'You're old, you know. You're gonna die soon.'"

"He did!" Lydia said.

"Just tell Dewey when the appointment is, that you're driving him, and not to worry, nobody thinks he's crazy. Whatever you do don't let him seduce you into arguing with him."

Frank looked at Lydia and grinned. "Lots of luck," he said.

"If you ignore him," I continued," he'll bluster a bit. At first it will be 'I'm not going so don't think I am,' but if you don't answer soon the story will change. It will become, 'OK I'll go, but I'm not talking, I just won't say one word.'"

"But what good will seeing him do if he doesn't talk?" Lydia asked.

"They all talk. Up-front kids like Dewey can't help it. In most cases I'm lucky to get a word in edgewise."

"I hope he doesn't just refuse to get out of the car," Lydia said, much doubt in her voice and manner.

I could see her uncertainty about bringing him might well encourage Dewey to stronger resistance, so I suggested, "Maybe his father should bring him. It doesn't matter who brings him."

"Could it be on a Saturday?" Frank asked. "I have trouble getting away weekdays."

So we set it up for Saturday next when Frank can bring him. Lydia seemed surprised and a little pleased that Frank was willing to handle this part of things.

"Can you make it eleven o'clock," Frank said. "He might forgive you for being what you are, but you make him miss Spiderman and you're done for."

"Oh, Frank," Lydia said. "Spiderman hasn't been around for at least a year now."

I laughed. I noticed that, now getting him here is Frank's problem, he's a little more interested in the details.

However, I was not really concerned about what Dewey missing TV will do to the interview to come. If he refuses to get out of the car, I'll go down and interview him there. For school phobia kids I've made home visits. So we arranged the appointment for eleven the following Saturday.

The Interview

Dewey arrived at eleven the next Saturday. By the time I came out to the waiting room to get him, he was immersed in a Charlie Brown book. He looked up briefly when I come in, avoided my gaze, and returned to his book. I can see he's nervous, but cool.

I waved goodbye to my previous patient, an equally cool nine-year-old girl, who surveyed Dewey with a practised eye. She gave me a wave. "So long, Frog," she said, flouncing out the door. I'm not French, but I am a little corrugated about the face and dome.

Her mother shrugged, looked at me over her glasses, and minced after her daughter. Being a child psychiatrist is really a lot of fun; every kid is a fresh adventure.

I noticed that Dewey wasn't really reading; he was watching things. When he looked up at me to catch my reaction to being called "frog," I caught his eye. He frowned and raised the book until it hid his face.

"This must be Dewey," I said to Frank. Dewey doesn't look up. "Come on into my playroom, Dewey." I turned to Frank, "We'll be at least forty-five minutes. Why don't you go get a cup of coffee?"

Father gave me an 'I've done my share' look, said "see ya later, Dewey," and stood up. I waved him out. Dewey lowered his book and uncertainly watched him go.

"Come on," I said, and led the way into the playroom. I did not look back. I knew he wasn't right behind me, but it's a rare kid who can, starting dead cold, defy that early in the game. I was reasonably sure he'd follow. And if he didn't, I'd handle the situation somehow.

As I went I chattered a bit, as though assuming he was right behind me. I entered the playroom and turned. As I did so he arrived in the playroom door.

Dewey's an open-faced, nice-looking boy with dark eyes and chestnut brown hair. He was wearing blue cords, colorful Adidas runners and a Blue Jays T-shirt. Within him curiosity was warring with cool; I could see he was interested in the models and toys on my shelves but, since it was his game plan to be uncooperative, he was in a bind. Perhaps he decided that was my fault too, for he gave me a sullen look and stood there turning his head slowly from side to side, like El Toro taking in the sunlit plaza.

With a sweep of an imaginary cape I indicated the far chair, the one facing the door. I have found kids feel better if the escape route is visible. "Have a seat," I said.

Dewey looked at me. I detected a hint of uncertainty in that casual armor of his. He sauntered over to the other chair, slid into it, and began fingering a plastic dinosaur handy on the play table.

"My name is Dr. Millar," I sat down opposite him. I took out my pad and wrote his name. "And you're Dewey. How old are you Dewey?"

I knew his age, but when kids are a bit anxious, it helps to start with a really easy question.

He looked at me as though considering whether answering one question was violating the oath of silence he had taken with respect to our interview. I smiled as though ignorant of his contrary status.

"Nine," he said.

"Nineteen," I repeated, and wrote down that number.

"Nine," Dewey said emphatically as though humoring the deaf.

"You sure don't look nineteen," I shook my head.

"I'm nine, I said!"

"Oh, nine. That's better. You'd never pass for nineteen you know." I scratched out my nineteen I'd written.

"You knew," Dewey said, giving me a suspicious look. "My Mom told you."

"Yeah!" I smiled. "She said you go to Brookside School and times tables is your favorite subject."

"I hate times tables," Dewey said. "She didn't tell you that."

"As a matter of fact," I said with a grin, "she said you don't like them at all; in fact she said you hate them."

"Times tables are stupid. Kids shouldn't have to learn them," Dewey challenged. "Every kid should just be given a calculator and never mind stupid times tables."

I know a couple of school principals who would agree with him, but since that wasn't relevant, I asked him, "What's two times two?"

He looked at me with contempt. "Four."

"Mathematical genius," I said, writing it down in my notes.

Dewey almost laughed but caught himself in time. He settled back in his chair. "How come you got all those models?"

"Kids make them."

"How come they don't take them home?"

"They're not finished. Some of the boys who see me every week like to build models. When they finish them they take them home."

"I'm not coming every week," Dewey announced.

"And you didn't want to come today either," I said.

"They made me."

"I know exactly what you said to your Dad on the way over here."

Dewey thought that over a moment, then challenged me. "Oh yeah! What?"

"You said, 'OK, I'll come, but I'm not talking. I'm not saying one word.'"

"How did you know that?" Dewey asked, suspicion in his gaze.

"I can read minds."

"Oh yeah!" Dewey scoffed.

"As a matter of fact, I can tell you what you are thinking this very minute."

He looked at me uncertainly.

"You're thinking, 'This guy can't read minds.'"

Dewey looked startled for a moment, then grinned. "Aw, that's just what anybody would think. You can't read minds."

I shrugged as though to say, I guess this kid is just too smart for me.

"I saw a guy on TV once that could bend real coins with his mind," Dewey said. "But they musta faked it. When the camera was turned away they coulda bent it with pliers."

I could see that Dewey's not overly trusting of adults.

He looked around the room and asked, "How come kids paint their models?"

"So they look more real. I help them."

He walked over to the shelves, "I bet I could paint a model as good as that." He picked up one of the models.

I walked over and gently took the model from him. "The boy has been working hard on that and they break easily, so I think we'd better not handle it."

Dewey shrugged, "I could build better'n that."

Being on his feet, he started wandering about, following wherever his eye led him. He flitted, getting the surface information, then drifting on to the next attractive color or interesting shape. Spoken to, he did not reply. Even if I asked him a question, unless the subject interested him, he let it dangle. His unresponsiveness now had more the quality of indifference than resistance. I played a few games with it, and it soon became clear that Dewey was minimally aware of any social obligation to respond even with a closing "I don't know." Egocentric children simply do not perceive the social dilemma of their auditor left dangling when not answered.

I went back to my chair and watched him for a while, commenting occasionally, but content for the moment to see what he might produce spontaneously, now that I had defused his initial contrariness.

The initial phase of many first interviews goes much like this. The child, uncertain or contrary or a mixture of both, needs to be helped over his apprehension or negativism. I find it best to ignore these, to fool around with a little nonsense, show him enough of my style to amuse and reassure him.

Of course there are some children who refuse to come in from the waiting room. Rather than separate the child from the parent I usually detach the parent and see the child in the waiting room for the first few minutes. However, if a battle-of-wills becomes necessary, I have it. After all, such are frequently part of the problem, and the sooner the behavior appears in the office, the sooner we can go to work understanding and dealing with it.

Rarely do children remain sullen and uncommunicative throughout the entire interview, particularly not those suffering from the Omnipotent Child Syndrome; they have neither the patience nor the self-control to remain silent.

Even so, one has to work at communicating with children. It is not possible to interview them in the passive mode Sigmund Freud prescribed for adults. One has to set up communicative interaction, not just by asking questions but also by expressing provocative opinions or generating imaginative exchanges and, at the same time, not put words in the child's mouth. Each situation is different, and the child psychiatrist needs to acquire a repertoire of methods and develop ingenuity in utilizing these if he is to involve the child in useful communication.

The purpose of the diagnostic interview is not simply to obtain information about the child's inner life. While that data is useful, the child psychiatrist is primarily concerned with appraising the child's coping style. How does he deal with the world and himself? Does he cope, or is his one of the myriad non-coping or life avoidant styles? How does he handle his feelings? How much self-control has he? How fragile is that control? How tuned in is he? How perceptive? How obtuse? Is he open or closed? Naïve or suspicious? Burnt or trusting? Can he laugh? How sensitive is he to limitations placed upon his autonomy?

Children are neither able nor willing to answer questions about these things. Children don't come to the psychiatrist for help; they come because their parent has made them come. They aren't motivated to reveal themselves. In many cases they have an opposite feeling, that the psychiatrist is sticking his nose in their business without invitation. Unlike the adult patient, if time passes without communication it doesn't usually bother the child as much as it does the psychiatrist.

There are exceptions. I recall one loquacious seven-year-old who, after the usual initial resistance and fifteen minutes of increasingly informative banter, said, "Hey Doc, we've been fooling around long enough. We got to get down to talking about my problem."

"OK," I said. "What's your problem?"

"My problem," he replied, "is my mother. She won't do what I say."

Returning to the interview at hand, I decided the time had come to activate Dewey's coping style in order to get a better look at it.

The best way to activate a coping style is to give it something with which to cope. I could of course precipitate an authoritative encounter; the history makes it clear such would undoubtedly produce interesting reactions. However, I prefer this kind of thing not take place too early in the interview.

There are reasons for this. In the first place, once you get into a battle-of-wills, even a trivial one, the rest of the child's pattern tends to become obscured, and the child can come out looking a whole lot more willful and contrary than he really is. In the second place, if most of the interview has been fairly non- threatening, one is better set up for a return visit should a treatment plan emerge from the evaluation. So I watched for an opportunity to intrude myself on Dewey.

At that moment Dewey sat down at the table. He had found a bottle of split-shot fishing weights which I use to weigh down the nose wheel on model airplanes. "What are these for?" he asked.

"Let me see," I said, holding out my hand. Dewey handed them over to me. I poured some out on the table. I picked one up and started examining it.

"These are turn-to-animal pills," I said. "If I give you the right one, I can turn you into any animal you want to be."

Dewey gave me a here-we-go-again look and sat back in his chair. "Those are fishing weights."

"They look like fishing weights," I admitted, "but they are really pills. Of course they only work for a week, but it's nice having a holiday from being a person for a week . . . birds don't have to go to school, you know."

"But they get shot at by hunters," Dewey said, spilling out some more weights. He began arranging them in rows. "I wouldn't want to be a bird."

"What would be the most fun to be?"

Dewey gave me a suspicious look. "Nothing. It wouldn't be fun to be nothing."

"OK," I replied, deciding to come in the back door. "What would be the worst animal to have to be?"

Dewey thought a moment. "A dinosaur. They're extinct." He looked up from arranging weights. "But if I was, I'd be the only one in the world. Everybody would want to come and see me."

"You'd be the most powerful creature in the world," I pointed out.

A wicked look came into Dewey's eye. "I could go over to Brookside School and stomp a few classrooms I know."

I shook my head. "Dinosaurs on the monkey bars!"

"Old Grant would throw a spazz," Dewey chuckled.

"Probably wouldn't be too pleased," I agreed.

"I'd be a Tyrannosaurus Rex. A huge one, with big teeth. A Tyrannosaurus Rex could throw a whole elementary school clear across the road you know."

"Then they couldn't have school," I objected. "That'd be terrible."

Dewey snorted derisively. "School is the dumbest place going."

He went on to give me a four-minute dissertation on the evils of education, a dissertation that ranged from his opinion of the curriculum,old fashioned and irrelevant in this age of calculators, recesses, too short, to the teaching staff, assembled, he was sure, for the purpose of ruining kids' days with their bossy and demanding ways. Somehow he ended on the subject of field trips.

"Kids got rights you know. I could call the social worker, you know; Teachers can't take away kids' rights to go on field trips."

"I heard Miss Grant wouldn't let you go because you didn't finish your math."

"My mom told you that, didn't she?" Dewey said with narrowed eyes; clearly Mother was going to hear more about this betrayal of his privacy.

"Actually I read her mind."

"She told you," Dewey declared.

"You're right. She told me," I confessed. "She and your dad told me all about the ways things are at school as well as home. About the problems like finishing your school work and getting dressed in the mornings. They told me about things because they're worried about you."

"They don't need to worry about me," Dewey said. "There's nothing wrong with me. When can I go home? Isn't the time up yet?" He looked at the door as though considering bolting.

I showed him my watch. "Our appointment is for forty-five minutes. We've got twenty-five left."

"Twenty-five minutes!" Dewey shouted. "Maybe your watch has stopped!" He looked at the door again.

Hoping to deflect our battle-of-wills for a little longer I tried to change the subject. "I see you're right-handed," I said. "Are you right-eyed too?"

"Boy! This is borrrring!" Dewey said.

"Most people are right-eyed."

"What do ya mean right-eyed? I don't write with my eye."

"Right, not write," I declared with a little mock indignation. "People see best with their right or left eye." I said. "I'm right-eyed."

"Whoop-de-do!"

"You're probably right-eyed too."

"Oh yeah! How can you tell?"

I rolled a sheet of paper into a tube. "Look at my nose through this telescope and you'll see which you are."

Uncertainly, he took the paper and sighted it on my nose. He was holding the tube to his right eye.

"See," I said, "You used your right eye."

"I could have used the left if I'd wanted to."

"Try!" I could see he was cooling down again. I watched him fumble the tube to his left eye and then close his right eye with his free hand. "At least seven out of every eight kids in your class are right-eyed. Did you know that?"

"Big deal," Dewey said.

"Here," I handed him my pencil and the pad with the notes on it. "Try writing with your left hand."

He took a stab at writing with his left hand but he couldn't do much. By now he'd become pretty cool so I asked him, "Tell me, Dewey, what are the kids like at Brookside?"

"Aw, you know. Some finks. The girls are yucky. I'm third toughest in my grade."

"Who's first?"

"Trevor. You know Trevor?"

"Never heard of him." Even if I had, I would never have told Dewey. I don't want my patients teasing each other about going to the shrink.

Dewey looked disappointed. He was probably hoping to get something on Trevor.

"If this ruler," I said, picking it up from the table top, "was your class, and on this end was smart, and on this end was dumb, and all the kids in your class were on the ruler, where would you come?"

Dewey indicated a spot about one inch from the smart end. "Cathy is the smartest. But she does the dumb work," he added, as though this constituted some kind of cheating. "I don't do dumb stuff."

"What about popular?" I asked. "If this end was the kid everybody liked most and this end was the worst, where'd you come?"

"That would be old Pampers down there," Dewey said pointing to the worst end. "Her name is Pam, but she acts like a baby so we call her Pampers. She doesn't like it. Sometimes she cries. What a baby!" Dewey's disgust was boundless.

"And where do you come?" I asked again.

"Oh, about the middle," Dewey said.

"They got a nickname for you, Dewey?"

"Everybody's got a nickname."

"What's yours?"

"It's just because it rhymes."

Since he was beginning to look a little uncomfortable I decided not to pursue the matter further. However, Dewey chose to.

"Some of the kids call me Screwy, but that's just because it rhymes. I don't care. That Trevor's the really screwy one; he thinks he's tough. When the teacher leaves the room he takes over and bosses everybody."

Gradually a picture of his peer relationships emerged. While he wasn't a scapegoat he was certainly taking some teasing, and he had begun, as so many of these children do, to expect things to go sour. Preferring to be the rejecter rather than the rejectee, he was starting his days bristling in anticipation.

"Every class has a Trevor," I said. "And a Pampers. And a smart girl like Cathy."

"I don't mind Cathy," Dewey protested. "She's OK. For a girl."

"Would you like me to turn you into a girl, Dewey?"

"No way!"

"You could have Barbies and everything, "I said with a grin.

"Yuck!"

Now that Dewey had become a little sunny it became apparent how negative his usual style had grown to be. All things being equal, any conversation with Dewey was liable, at the turn of a phrase, to fall into a push-pull kind of interaction. All that was needed was for you to take a stand. If you said black, Dewey would say white. The closest to agreement you could ever expect from Dewey would be dark gray.

I managed to get him talking about his interests and found he was filled with grandiose fantasies involving various superheroes. His accounts were shot through with the theme of naked and overwhelming power.

I drew pictures for him of people whose faces I filled in to his specifications.

"Make him mad," he said. "He's mad because they made him go to bed and his favorite show was just coming on." He then elaborated on the ways that the kid is going to get even and became quite heated as he warmed to his subject.

"They try to do that to me, but I sneak out and watch from the door. I don't see why kids have to go to bed; grown-ups get to stay up." I gave him some felt pens and as he talked he drew me a picture, a poster advocating Kid Power.

Distantly I heard the waiting room door close. Since it was undoubtedly Dewey's father returning, I carried on. "Tell me, Dewey, have you thought about what you want to be when you grow up?"

"I'm going to be in the army and drive a tank," Dewey said. "Or maybe fly a jet." He stood up. "I think that was my father."

I nodded. "I think so."

"I'll go check," Dewey said.

"No need. I told him forty-five minutes. He knows to wait."

"I'll just tell him," Dewey said, standing up.

"That isn't necessary, Dewey." I indicated for him to sit down.

"Why can't I go now?" Dewey demanded, not sitting down.

"Because we're not finished. It'll only be a few minutes more." It was clear that Dewey was determined to set up a battle but I tried to deflect him.

"Come on Dewey, sit down and tell me about your grandfather. Your mother says he sometimes takes you fishing."

"I'm not sitting down," Dewey said, sidling towards the door.

I stood up and moved my chair into the path toward the door. "I guess you don't have to sit down if you don't want to."

Dewey looked at me uncertainly. "How much longer did you say?"

I checked my watch. "About four minutes."

"You let me go in two, and I'll sit down," he offered.

As Frank said, all Dewey wants is to win. I wouldn't mind excepting it wouldn't be good for him. Already I know I am going to suggest treatment to the family, so sooner or later Dewey and I are going to have to sort out what adults decide and what kids decide. Part of growing him up is going to be confronting his omnipotence illusion. If I compromise now, the next round will be that much harder.

"You don't have to sit down if you'd rather stand."

"But what about my two minutes? You didn't answer me about that," Dewey said, walking toward the toy shelves.

"The time you leave is not your decision. It's mine. It's only a few minutes now and then you can go. What are you going to do when you leave?"

"None of your damn business," Dewey snapped.

"Dam business? I don't have any business with dams. I'm not a water man."

"Funny!"

Clearly Dewey was caught up in the power struggle, and it didn't look as if my efforts to help him save face were going to be effective.

"I'm never coming back you know," Dewey said. "This is a dumb place. You're a dumb doctor."

I decided any words from me now would just aggravate the situation, so I remained silent.

"How much longer now?" Dewey asked loudly.

I checked my watch. "Two minutes."

Dewey grabbed a model from the shelf and held it over his head. "You'd better let me go," he shouted.

I stood up. "Dewey! Don't you break that model!"

Dewey dropped the model on the shelf and ran across the room. "If you hit me I'm telling."

"I'm not going to hit you, Dewey," I said, picking up the model and checking it. "But neither am I going to let you leave until the time is up. There are some things you decide and some I decide, and when the appointment is over is one I decide."

Dewey turned his back to me and stared out the window. He remained there saying nothing until, two minutes later, I opened the door for him and told him he could leave. He rocketed through it like a scalded cat. He continued straight through the waiting room waving at his father to follow.

As I entered the waiting room Frank stood and looked at me inquiringly.

I shrugged. "We ended in a little battle-of-wills."

"I heard," Frank said. "Sorry."

"Don't worry," I grinned. "We'll both survive."

Additional Information

The next day, after getting the parents' permission to do so, I called Miss Grant. I was relieved to discover she was happy to talk to me. Some teachers aren't. By and large she confirmed the picture of Dewey the parents had given me.

It was my impression that Miss Grant had been quite patient, not particularly indulgent of Dewey, and that she had varied her approach considerably in an effort to find some way to deal with his recalcitrance, but that nothing had worked. At this point she seemed strongly motivated to prove how impossible a child Dewey was, more as a defense of her teaching than as a rejection of the child.

Sometimes teachers can get into continuing power struggles with kids and become part of the problem, but this was not the case here.

Since there was no indication of any real disability for learning, I did not feel psychological testing was necessary to clarify the diagnosis. Nor was there reason to suspect a neurological component so such a consultation was not necessary.

Diagnostic Formulation

These data then are the main facts from which the child psychiatrist must formulate his understanding: what he learns from and of the parents; what he learns from direct contact with the child; and what he learns from others having significant contact with the child. To be sure, when circumstances warrant, it may be necessary to undertake special medical studies, such as a neurological examination, a brain wave test, or psychological studies. However, in the usual case, the history and the direct examination of the child provide the significant findings.

Let me now offer a brief explanation of what is going on with Dewey. It will take the book to complete the job, but it would be inappropriate to leave the case history without giving some preliminary indication of the relationship of its elements one to another.

Dewey has a lot of symptoms. He avoids duties and responsibilities both at home and at school. He can't get along with kids, and he isn't easy to live with at home either. He's willful, contrary and sometimes rude. He has poor self-control for a nine year old, as his tears and tantrums show. His bragging covers an uncertain sense of his own worth. If he trusted his parents more he wouldn't still be plagued with anxiety whenever they separate from him.

These symptoms and qualities are best understood in terms of that pattern of adaptive immaturity I call the Omnipotent Child Syndrome. There are four central or cardinal characteristics of the syndrome.

THE CARDINAL CHARACTERISTICS
The Omnipotence Illusion
Egocentricity
Intolerance for Unpleasure
Impaired Self Esteem

Dewey has not found a way to accept his childhood, to give up his illusion of omnipotence for a belief in his parents' power and good will towards him. He struggles to deny his real childhood, which leads him into willfulness and the conviction that authority is there to demean, not to protect and nurture him.

Dewey is self-centered to the point that he regularly misreads his environment in terms of self. His insensitivity is such that he offends and doesn't realize what he has done to generate offense. He is not so much selfish as imperceptive. Like the four year old, he believes that, when he closes his eyes, it's night for the rest of the world.

Dewey has limited ability to tolerate the normal unpleasures of child life. He wants it now. If it's no fun, take it away. Minimal anxiety fells him. Disappointment overwhelms. Anger erupts. There is no restraint in Dewey. He has not developed the capacity to contain unpleasure.

Finally Dewey has little sense of worth. His self-esteem is fragile, and a good deal of his unacceptable behavior results because he is trying to force others to endorse a worth he does not feel within himself.

Dewey's adaptive growth has faltered. He is trying to cope with a nine year old's world with the adaptive equipment of a four year old. If he is unhappy, it is because such incompetence leads to repeated failures. His emotional conflict is a result of his condition, not its cause.

Why has Dewey's adaptive growth not proceeded well? When we look into the history we do not see parents who have withheld affection and concern; instead we see parents who have not found a way to train their child. They have nurtured adequately, but they have disciplined poorly.

At this point my clinical task is to meet with the parents and explain Dewey's condition to them. Then we must make a plan to catch up the lost ground, to set Dewey's growth in motion again. We must devise ways to deal with each aspect of Dewey's adaptive growth failure: his residual omnipotence, his egocentricity, his impatience, and his defective self-esteem.

The next four chapters will be devoted to examining each of these characteristics individually. Each chapter will begin with a clinical description of the particular characteristic in action. Then the other ways in which that particular characteristic commonly manifests itself will be recounted.

From the clinical picture we shall then move to a developmental perspective, first describing the process of normal psychological development with respect to the given cardinal characteristic. How does infantile omnipotence normally give way to the comfortable acceptance of rational authority? How does the egocentric toddler become a reasonably perceptive and accommodative child? How do patience and persistence develop? How is self- esteem constructed?

This leads us naturally into a discussion of parenting techniques aimed at promoting and/or remediating each element of adaptive growth. Each chapter will end with a detailed program of management of the clinical example with which we began the chapter.

Let us turn now to our first such chapter, a discussion of infantile omnipotence.

2

The Omnipotence Illusion

The three year old was sitting in her high chair feeding herself. She dug her spoon into the cooked cereal, stirred it about a moment, grinned at her mother, then conveyed an unstable load to the approximate vicinity of her mouth. After managing to insert a little less than fifty percent of the porridge into her mouth, she leaned her head against the chair back, chubby arm along the tray, spoon at parade rest, and surveyed her kingdom. Her eyes seemed calculating as she munched and cogitated.

Without warning, she raised her spoon to the vicinity of her right ear and threw it to the floor. "Pick it up," she ordered her startled mother.

"That wasn't nice, Pammy," Mother said as she retrieved the spoon, wiped and returned it.

Pammy looked at the spoon. She looked at her mother a moment, then once more raised the spoon to the vicinity of her ear and gracefully lobbed it across the room. "Pick it up," she ordered loudly.

At this point most mothers might have tried to amuse or distract Pammy from her provocative agenda, but Pammy's mother didn't. She retrieved the spoon once more, wiped it on her apron, and returned it with a warning. "Throw it again, and I won't pick it up."

Pammy inspected the spoon a moment, glanced at her mother in a sidelong fashion, then raised the spoon in the vicinity of her right ear once more. She paused a moment, looking at her mother, who said nothing. Pammy frowned and hurled the spoon across the room. "Pick it up!" she shouted.

"No way." Mother, who had been through the *battle-of-wills* bit before, got up from her chair and walked over to the kitchen counter where she busied herself putting things away.

Pammy threw a tantrum. She shoved her cereal bowl off the end of her tray, slid down in her chair, arms above her head, until the retaining strap halted her. There she stuck, yelling loudly and angrily.

After a few seconds Mother took Pammy from her chair and carried her, struggling, to her room and deposited her in her crib. Then, closing the bedroom door, Mother left Pammy to holler.

Pammy yelled constantly for four minutes. Much of it was shouting commands to the effect that her mother should attend her majestic presence immediately. When these were ignored her tone became more complaining that imperious. Soon she was uttering intermittent yelps, which gradually became woebegone in tone.

Mother went to Pammy's room and picked her from her crib. She ignored the brief resurgence of vocal indignation and carried Pammy back to her high chair. Then she did something many mothers would hesitate to do: she gave Pammy another bowl of porridge and her spoon.

She challenged her.

Pammy looked at the porridge. She looked at her mother. She picked up the spoon. She looked at her mother again. Mother returned her gaze calmly, saying nothing. Pammy raised the spoon to the vicinity of her right ear. Still Mother said nothing. Then, deciding her head was itchy, and the spoon was an ideal implement for the job, Pammy began scratching behind her right ear.

What we have here is a typical battle-of-wills which three year olds are famous for. The only atypical thing is that Mother won, but then this was her fourth child and she had been around this mulberry bush before.

Battles-of-wills are normal events in early childhood, inevitable once the parent starts to intrude upon the infant's self-appointed agenda. The toddler struggles to preserve the omnipotence illusion which has been the principal source of his security. But the magnitude of his realistic helplessness cannot be denied much longer. He battles to preserve the illusion, but it is a struggle he must lose if he is to overcome his separation anxiety, give up *magic* for realistic coping skills and develop trust

The happiest way to traverse the pre-adolescent years is for the child to come to feel secure in the shelter of his parents' authority. This means giving up the omnipotence illusion for a belief in the parents' power. When this happens, in time the child comes to experience parental limits and expectations not as put-downs or denigrations but as evidence of mother's concern for his or her well-being.

It certainly does not seem this way to the child faced with the prospect of surrendering his throne. To him the situation seems desperate. To him it seems you are either a king or a slave; either you give the orders or you get ordered about. There is no place in the small child's understanding for autonomy, the notion that he has a right to a degree of self-determination appropriate to his maturity.

In order for the child to give up his omnipotence illusion, his parents need to set effective limits in a few crucial areas. For his sake the parents need to win a few battles-of-wills. They do not need to overwhelm the child with their authority. They need to leave room for him to make a few choices. "You may wear the red socks or the green, but you cannot go without socks." "You may wash first and dress second, if you wish, but you have to do both before you come down."

If parents err on the side of indulgence, the child will retain his omnipotence illusion, because it is possible to do so. If they come down on the side of over control, he will struggle harder, for his fear that he is about to be inducted into slavery will seem well-founded.

Planful firmness about a few items, coupled with leaving him a few choices, treads the middle ground and works better.

These days, more parents err on the side of permissiveness than control The result of this is evident throughout the society. One has only to keep one's eye open to observe even adults engaged in interpersonal encounters which have the same basic characteristic as throwing their spoon to the floor.

If parents have trouble setting limits and communicating expectations, their child is liable to have trouble navigating the omnipotence-devaluation phase of adaptive growth. When this happens, progress is not made and the struggle continues. This is manifest at home, and surfaces in the child psychiatrist's office in a variety of ways.

Manifestations of Retained Omnipotence

Parents complain that their eight-year-old child does not obey: "He won't do what he is supposed to do"; "He just ignores you when you ask him to do something"; "He won't do his homework, and I can't get him to do it." He may not always refuse but instead finds ways to avoid, ignore, and/or resist.

Duties, chores, anything the child experiences as tedious, the child won't do unless he is constantly supervised, and when one undertakes such supervision, battles-of-wills ensue.

Of course no child likes to do tedious things, but there is a difference between the child who is simply avoiding unpleasure and the child who feels his right to be totally self-determining is being threatened. The avoidant child, when pressed, grumbles but complies. He accepts that his parent or teacher has the right to expect things of him.

Not so the omnipotent child. He reacts to increased pressure with less compliance rather than more. "The more you press him, the more he gets his back up," mothers report. It's as though the pressure changes the subject. The issue is no longer, "I don't want to do that because it's no fun." It now becomes, "Who do you think you are telling me what to do?" or "You're not the boss of me, I don't have to do what you say." In such cases a battle-of- wills develops.

Some mothers report, "I've learned the best way to get him to do something is to make him think it is his idea," which of course is to defer to his omnipotence illusion.

Even though mothers try to go round his end, the disobedience often escalates to defiance and, if this particular mother is uncertain or paralyzed by guilt, she may find herself the principal subject of an omnipotent tyrant.

The fact is the child does not accept that the parent has the right to require something of him. Such children feel there is no special prerogative of parenthood and often they say so. "You and Dad get to stay up late, so why can't I?" Explanations that involve any differences in the rights of parent and child are rejected out of hand.

Some children are fiercely omnipotent. They seek to rule their families, most particularly their mothers, and they react violently to obstruction.

One mother described her eleven year old as follows: "He **wants** to rule, everything has to be his way. He bosses us all. If I try to be firm and make him do what he is supposed to do he has a tantrum. He abuses me. He calls me stupid. He sometimes spits in my face. He insists on doing what he wants. He won't go to bed at night. He never brushes his teeth, and once when I tried to insist, he ran out of the house and didn't come back until after supper. If there's something at school he doesn't want to face, like a test, he just refuses to go, and he's too big for me to carry to the car."

Another mother described her nine year old's behavior as follows: "He's a tyrant, he tells me what to do and if I don't do it that very minute he screams and yells at me. He won't let me talk on the telephone. He insists I hang up, and he screams until I do. I'm his slave," she concluded morosely.

Another mother described similar overbearing and demanding behavior from her ten-year-old daughter. "If I don't do what she wants she threatens to kill herself, to put her finger into the light socket, or to run out in front of a truck. Twice now she's taken a knife from the kitchen drawer and threatened to stick it in herself. What can I do? She's just wild enough to do it when she gets like that."

Sometimes similar manifestations at school are the reason for referral to my office. One child refused to remain in his seat when the teacher told him to, and when she tried to put him out in the hall, he climbed out onto the second story window sill and threatened to jump. This same child revealed the pervasive nature of his omnipotence illusion on another occasion when the teacher announced she had compiled a list of children who were to remain after school and finish their work. Although the child's name was not on the list, he was so offended by the teacher's assumption of authority that he took the list from her desk, tore it up, and deposited it in the waste basket. When he was finally escorted to the principal's office he reacted by "firing" the principal. When the principal ignored his pink slip, the child declared his intention of taking the matter to the Board of Education.

Amusing as some of this behavior may seem, these children are in earnest. They cherish their omnipotence illusion, and when it is challenged they defend it.

Dramatic examples make the omnipotence illusion obvious, but sometimes it is less openly expressed. One child, for example, would not start his class work without several reminders. Eventually, after much pressure, he wrote his name but nothing else. When further pressed he completed the work-sheet but left out all the capital letters on the words.

What he was doing was refusing the teacher's authority in his own fashion. Though he complied superficially, he pretended to himself that, by making changes in the work. he was not really doing it. He did not do what the teacher ordered, he did what he decided to do.

Maintaining the omnipotence illusion requires not only that others not expect the child to obey them but also that they obey the child. So it is that the omnipotent child sets out to run the household. If he had his way, and some try mightily to do so, every morning he would hand each family member his or her agenda for the day.

The omnipotent child seeks to dominate playtime and often alienates his peers with his bossiness. When this leads to rejection, omnipotent children often end up playing with younger children who will let them lead, or with a passive child on the social fringe who has to take whom he can get.

When omnipotent children play games they are always the teacher, the general, the chief. When they cannot be, they storm and threaten. If this does not work they withdraw from the game, go home and watch TV.

Attempts to boss outside adults meet with less success, but the omnipotent child often achieves a surprising degree of control over his family. He is frequently deferred to. "It's easier than fighting with him," his mother says with a shrug. So he sends back his dinner and Mother makes him a sandwich. Or she fishes his favorite shirt out of the laundry and irons it at the last minute in time for school.

One frequent manifestation of the omnipotence illusion occurs in a form of an interaction I call role swapping. In order to deny his mother's parental prerogative, the child reacts to her expression of it by assuming the identical prerogative himself. Mother says, "I'll punish you," and the child responds, "No, I'll punish you." And he finds a way to do it. The teacher prepares an assignment for the children, and the child prepares an assignment of his own, so assuming the prerogatives of the teacher.

In my playroom I run into the same thing. A seven-year-old girl of the imperious persuasion attended my playroom recently. Late in the interview she observed my notes from my previous interview with her parents and she asked what those were.

"Those are my notes," I replied. "Your mom and dad were in telling me about your family, and I wrote some of it down so I wouldn't forget."

"About me?" Susie asked suspiciously.

"Some about you," I replied.

"Let me see!"

"They're not typed yet. You couldn't read my writing."

She looked into the file and decided I was right, as I knew she would. Even I can't read my writing if I leave the matter over three days.

She picked up a pencil and a piece of paper and said, "I'll keep notes about you. Did you have an unhappy childhood, Dr. Millar?"

When it was time to go I got up, went to the playroom door and called back to her, "It's time to go, Susie." She looked up from her notes, shook her head and, with a little grin, said, "Send in the next patient."

Implicit in role swapping is the rejection of the difference in prerogatives between the child-parent, child-teacher, child-doctor, which is, of course, a manifestation of the retained omnipotence illusion.

Some omnipotent children state their views about the distribution of power quite openly, as the following common quotes illustrate:

"You're not the boss. I don't have to do what you say."

"It's my room, I'll keep it dirty if I want."

"No second grade teacher is going to boss me about."

"I'm not your maid, you know."

"Kids should be the bosses."

"I don't have to take this, I can go live by myself."

Many children accuse the limit setter of being mean and bossy. They are particularly fond of the "Hitler" epithet. Some children threaten dire consequences if the adult persists in his or her unfair assumption of boss power. They utter threats such as, "When I grow up I'm going to shoot you." Or, if the offending boss be a teacher, "I'll bring dynamite and blow up the school."

More sophisticated children generate more subtle anti-authoritian gambits. "I'm bringing a tape recorder to class and I'm going to hide it in my desk and make a record of how Old Crow yells at the kids, and then I'm taking it to the school board."

These maneuvers have a way of keeping up with the times; these days I hear a lot of talk from children about calling the child abuse line. This threat is supposed to generate instant adult deferment. Sometimes it does. Who isn't afraid of social workers these days?

The refusal of omnipotent children to accept adult authority is evident in other behaviors too. One seven-year-old child was out in the car driving with his father when they passed the state capital. "That's where they make the laws," his father said.

The child averted his eyes and would not look. Later, the child made it clear to me that he felt laws were unfair and he didn't want to acknowledge the presence of a whole building devoted to their creation.

Some children openly reject the notion of God's power, seeing this as an affront to their right to be wholly self-determining. However, they are not above invoking this power to put others in their place. "You're not the boss of this office," one seven year old told me when I had indicated to him that throwing toys was not acceptable. "God is."

The play of these children is often dominated by "power" themes. Children's television makes its living on power themes. It was ever thus, but fairy tales didn't rub our noses in it. Sure Jack climbed the beanstalk and killed the giant, but mostly he obeyed his mother. Check out the cartoons. If a child character isn't the Superhero, then he's a close friend of the hero who does what the child wills him to do. After growing up with cartoon heroes can you wonder that, when these children become teen-agers, some of them die their hair cartoon colors?

Some children become obsessed with a particular cartoon hero. A few years back I saw a child who would spend his entire play day enacting the role of the Six Million Dollar Man. Of course he was Steve Austin and the other children were either villains or menial henchmen. Furthermore, he would insist hotly that bionic power was real.

I am told that Hitler was addicted to American cowboy heroes when he was a child. Listen to the way that omnipotent child expressed his omnipotence. "One word I never recognized . . . in my battle for power: capitulation . . . that is the surrender of will to another person. Never! Never!"

Omnipotent children are absolutely determined to have their own way, and if they cannot bully their parents they learn to manipulate them. For example, most, sooner or later, learn that the phrase "You don't love me any more" is magically effective in dealing with resistant parents.

They learn also that threats to injure themselves are similarly effective. "I'm going to run out on the road and get hit by a car. I don't care what happens to me," is a maneuver that has a way of changing the subject between parent and child.

As one sees child after child caught up in this strong need to deny the realistic limitations of his power, one comes to recognizes that the omnipotence illusion is desperately important to these children.

Why?

It is not just that they want to avoid tedious duties. No! To them to accept their parents' authority is to acknowledge the realistic differences in the power of children and adults. This they find demeaning. They struggle valiantly to preserve the omnipotence illusion.

There is another reason too. Since they don't trust, they believe that only by controlling the world can they be safe in it. While this is a common view in three e year olds, it should pass and trust take its place. This has not happened for omnipotent children.

In order to understand and ultimately deal with this, let's now examine the normal course of omnipotence-devaluation in psychological growth.

The Omnipotence-Devaluation Phase

Although the newborn is wholly dependent upon others for his survival, he has no knowledge that this is his true state. The infant lives in a sea of feelings and ill-defined perceptions, which he cannot yet separate one from another. His state is, to quote St. Augustine, "a blooming, buzzing confusion." He feels cold and hunger. He sees light and hears noise, but he has as yet no well-defined self to tell him which sensation comes from within and which from without.

Hungry, he cries, and, somewhere from out of that vague sea, satisfaction in the form of food arrives. Once this happens a few times he begins to differentiate inner (hunger) from outer (satisfaction).

His first notion of power has to be one of omnipotence. He knows nothing of such factors as cows and milkmen, of stoves and mother love. All he knows is that he hollers, the bottle comes, and the sequence keeps happening.

In time he comes to identify his mother as a particular configuration in that external sea, a looming moon with two blue craters and a red lined cavity that makes cooing noises and is somehow associated with a variety of satisfactions. Even though he begins to realize she is not part of himself, he still be believes she is subject to his will. He cries and she comes; it must be because he cried. He is too immersed in self to conceive his mother as a separate individual with a choice in the matter.

He is possessed of the omnipotence illusion. It is an inevitable state of infancy. It protects the child from an appreciation of how truly helpless and vulnerable he is.

If the child knew how simply his care could be abandoned, how utterly dependent he is, he would be flooded with anxiety. But that realization is acquired slowly Furthermore, as it is acquired, he is becoming equipped with competencies that reduce his helplessness.

Once the child is on his feet, his disillusionment proceeds apace. He runs into natural laws such as the law of gravity. He tries to fly from a chair and thumps his forehead a good one. He scolds the floor, tells the rotten world what he thinks of it, but he doesn't try to fly again. Furthermore, he begins to learn something about power in the world.

Infants enjoy tweaking the nose of gravity. The denial of its power sometimes seems to motivate their play. If you hold an eighteen-month-old child on your shoulder and let him swing a heavy door with his hand he is delighted to move that enormous object by his force alone. He will play the game as along as you are prepared to hold him there. Similarly, balloons are appealing to small children, I think because they are large things that the child can move. Such play, for the moment, serves to deny the powerless state.

But there are more large things they can't move than large they can, so, despite balloons, disillusionment proceeds. Provided of course Mother allows such learning to proceed. I recall one mother telling me about her three year old who was immensely offended when the sofa wouldn't remove itself from his path when he ordered it to do so. He shoved it to no avail. He fell to the floor, kicking and banging in a temper tantrum. It took him fifteen minutes to get over his outrage. His mother, a sensitive caring woman who did not wish to see her child so traumatized, took to keeping an eye on his living room excursions, and when he approached the sofa she would crouch behind it so that when he pushed, she pulled, and the sofa did move, thus sparing her the trauma of witnessing his distress but doing nothing to disillusion his omnipotence.

On has to wonder if Mahomet's mother didn't do something similar. And how about that King Canute, ordering the ocean to retreat!

At the same time as his omnipotence is gradually being disillusioned, the child's awareness of the boundaries of self is increasing. Soon he separates his identity from that of his mother. Since she is the principal satisfier of his needs, the more separate he perceives her, the more necessary it is for him to assure himself she is subservient to his will.

Eventually he comes to recognizes her operant power, that she can move the world in ways that he cannot, but he does not recognize the independence of her will. He begins to see himself as the executive in charge. It is as though she were a robot and all her buttons were his to push as he wished. One articulate three year old expressed this most succinctly when he announced, "She's my mother. She has to do what I say."

As long as the child wins the battle-of-wills he is reassured. He is omnipotent. She does have to do what he says. The world is under his control, and all is well.

But, as we have seen, Mother gradually and naturally becomes less willing to defer to the child's demands. For one thing the demands are escalating, both in frequency and magnitude. Since the child is no longer just sleeping and eating, he intrudes upon her time much more than before. Indeed, most toddlers would have their mothers constantly at their side entertaining them. If Mother does not start denying the child occasionally, her life will no longer be her own.

Whether or not it results in a battle-of- wills, Mother is going to have to say no sometimes.

Furthermore, Mother is beginning to realize that she has another job to do besides simply nurturing the child. As she watches her tiny emperor cruising his kingdom, she realizes that others are not going to be willing to reorganize their lives for his benefit, that as soon as he ventures outside of the protection of home, he is going to have to do a little accommodating to others. And if she doesn't train him for this, nobody else is going to.

The Process of Disillusionment

So Mother begins the process of omnipotence disillusionment. She does not fetch his bottle so promptly as before. "It won't hurt him to wait while I heat it," she thinks. So she ignores his protests a little longer than before.

"Where's the damn bottle?" her child thinks. Well, maybe he doesn't swear; but only because he hasn't yet learned the words, not because he doesn't feel like it. He begins to get worried. "Wow," he thinks, "If she does not come when I call, who will feed and look after me?"

He has received a hint of his powerless condition and he rejects the input. "No way!" he declares. "She has to come when I call, and I'll just prove it." He hollers! She comes! "That's more like it," he assures himself, as that uneasy feeling settles in his breast.

What uneasy feeling? When he's older he'll recognize it as anxiety . For the moment let's call it the vague presentiment that his omnipotence might not be quite so absolute as he thought. He has received a hint of the truth of his situation, that he is wholly unable to fend for himself, that he is totally dependent upon his mother's care, which she might just withhold if she chooses to.

Tomorrow the whole sequence happens again, and the next day too. He begins to suspect that there is a leak in the boat of his omnipotence. To the omnipotent child this is bad news indeed; he needs her to fetch and carry! Holy diapers, Batman, what if she doesn't come at all? Who will feed me? Where is she? So it is that as omnipotence is challenged, separation anxiety arises.

The normal two year old does not take this kind of thing lying down. He fights back. Tthis is what the terrible twos are all about.

However, not every mother experiences a terrible twos with her toddler. Some children are so mild tempered, and the situation so low key, that omnipotence devaluation proceeds without much ruffling of the surface waters.

Sometimes, if this is Mother's first child and she has nothing else to do but serve him, she continues to obey her child's orders. Other times she is just too soft and caring to grasp the nettle. Sometimes, she is just a child herself, like Hitler's mother, and it is beyond her limited capacity to cope with this most difficult aspect of parenting.

However, in most families, when the heretofore sunny two year old becomes provocative and demanding, Mother recognizes the need to fight back. It's not easy. When he says, "I don't want Wheaties, I want Corn Flakes," and Mother brings Corn Flakes, now it's Rice Krispies he wants. Then back to Wheaties again. There is no satisfying him. Why? Because his agenda is to set up a battle-of-wills, win it, and preserve his endangered omnipotence illusion.

That may be his agenda, but it cannot be his parents', for the child's adaptive growth depends upon surrendering the omnipotence illusion and learning to trust. Mother cannot always pander; she must sometimes confront. Where does this take her? Of course! Into a battle-of- wills.

In lively, upfront children, battles-of-wills escalate into temper tantrums. Dealt with properly, the adaptive sequence I call omnipotence disillusionment is soon worked through. However, if it is not dealt with properly, the terrible twos can persist and become the terrible threes, fours, fives or even forties.

With pre-school children omnipotence-devaluation is a normal developmental process, much easier to handle then than it will be later. This is preventive parenting. With the eight year old we are into remedial parenting which, while not impossible, takes longer and is a lot harder.

Navigating the Normal Omnipotence-Devaluation Phase

The central event of the omnipotence-devaluation phase is the battle-of-wills. To be sure these may sometimes be avoided by finding a way to make the child think the solution you seek was really his idea. "Wouldn't it be fun to play in the bath now?" Or the child may seduced into compliance by such maneuvers as, "I'll race you to the table."

While the occasional use of such measures is justified, if they become mother's standard approach omnipotence-devaluation will not proceed. Unless the child takes matters into his own hands. Which they tend to do.

If a child really wants to have a battle-of-wills, it's almost impossible not to end obliging him. Let me illustrate this with an example in which I was personally involved.

One day a five-year-old child was brought to me by his mother. I led him into my playroom. He glowered at me. Clearly, he did not want to be here with me.

"You can play with anything you want," I said, waving at my toy shelf

"I wanna play with the blocks," he demanded.

I brought him the blocks.

"No!" said pushing the blocks aside. "I wanna play with the cars."

So I brought him the cars.

"Nope!" he shook his head. "I wanna play with the puppets."

I took away the cars and brought him the puppets. I had an idea what he was doing but I was curious to see how long he would keep it up, so I just smiled and fetched. We went though a couple of more items, fetched and refused. Each time his face grew darker and more angry.

Finally, terminally exasperated, he looked at me and shouted, "I wanna play with sumpin' you haven't got."

See what I mean?

Battles-of-wills may be won or lost with each participant defining those terms differently. Furthermore, each outcome has a very different impact on the child's adaptive development. Here are the scenarios of both winning and losing as I believe small children experience these events.

THE CHILD WINS
I'm all powerful, my mother obeys me.
She's not obeying me! I'm not all powerful?
Battle of wills leading to a temper tantrum
It worked. She obeyed me. I am all powerful.
Omnipotence intact.
Back to square one.

Obviously the child who wins a battle-of-wills has had his omnipotence illusion confirmed and so makes no adaptive progress. What of the other case?

THE ADULT WINS
I am all powerful. My mother obeys me.
She's not obeying me. I'm not all powerful?
Battle of wills leading to a temper tantrum.
She didn't obey me. I'm not all powerful.
Doom and Gloom!
Adaptive development given a nudge.
Square two next time out.

The key, of course, is winning the battle of wills by managing the temper tantrum. We'll come back to this later.

Doom and gloom is a sad state of being and it is not surprising that the child struggles against it with vim and vigor. But doom is an unreal appreciation of his situation. True, he is weak and powerless and he cannot control his mother, but in the normal family he is valued, indeed of great worth in his parents' eyes.

He will be fed and looked after. Perhaps not so promptly as he demands, but with care and concern. Most important of all, Mother doesn't leave him. She is there in the morning when he wakes.

There is no way for the child to appreciate this reality except by experiencing it. The child who loses a battle-of-wills and discovers that his needs are met anyway begins to realize that his apprehensions are groundless. This reduces the magnitude of his separation anxiety. It also disillusionsions his omnipotence. "Maybe she doesn't fetch the moment I call," he tells himself, "but she comes eventually." Soon this becomes, "Maybe I can't make Mother do what I want but I can count on her doing what I need."

When the child surrenders his omnipotence illusion, he exchanges it for another illusion, a belief in his parents' omnipotence. Mother is all powerful. She can heal hurts with a kiss or a laying on of hands. She can tame teachers, intimidate principals, and fire governors if necessary. Father is the strongest father on the block. He can lift cars by the bumper if he wants to. Just as the child once over-valued his power, now he over-values his parents' power. And he will do so until adolescence upsets this particular apple-cart.

The child has found a new equation for security. Perhaps **he is no longer the king, but he is a close friend of the king,** and he is going to be all right. To live in the shadow of the king frees the child. No longer does he have power worries, his energies are freed for growth. He can spend his days acquiring adaptive strength and building his persona while others take care of his security.

The mother who continues to defer to her child when she should be standing up to him is not only perpetuating his illusion with respect to the distribution of power but is also robbing her child of the chance to learn to trust, condemning him to a life in which he must control his world to feel safe in it.

Once the child surrenders his omnipotence illusion, a number of unseen benefits accrue. Principal among these is that the door to trust now opens.

The Genesis of Trust

Let us consider how successful navigation of the omnipotence-devaluation phase leads to the capacity for trust.

As every suspicious husband knows, you don't have to trust those whom you can control. So it is not until the child recognizes that he can't control his mother that her continued care of him can generate trust.

It is conventional wisdom that all that is necessary for a child to learn to trust the world is that he receive regular and loving care. This is not so. Over the years I have seen many concerned and caring parents who have provided regular and loving care but whose children have developed very little trust. The problem in these cases has not been a lack of love but a failure to disillusion the child's omnipotence such that he comes to realize his parents care for him because they love him, not because they are subject to his omnipotent will.

It is not possible to overestimate the importance of the successful disillusionment of infantile omnipotence. People who must live their lives devoid of trust in their fellow man surely tread the lowest byways of this vale of tears.

How then is trust related to omnipotence devaluation? The sequence goes like this. When the child loses a battle-of-wills, he finds he cannot control his mother. But his security has always depended upon the illusion that he could. He becomes insecure. "If I can't control her, what if she doesn't feed and care for me? She could leave. I could starve. Where is she?"

So it that the first effect of omnipotence disillusionment is that it leads to anxiety, most particularly a form that has come to be known as *separation anxiety*.

But what is the subsequent reality? The child is still fed and looked after. Perhaps not so promptly as he would wish, but he is looked after. What does this tell the child? It tells him that his anxiety is groundless. It leads him to another view. "Maybe I can't make her do what I want," he realizes, "but I can count on her doing what I need." So is trust born.

So long as the child believes he is king, he cannot come to trust. It isn't until he accepts that he cannot control his mother that he can learn to trust her.

Here, in summary form, is a brief recapitulation of this crucial sequence.

THE GENESIS OF TRUST
STAGE 1
Firm limits ---> Loss of omnipotence illusion
Child realizes dependency
Separation anxiety develops
STAGE 2
Mother meets needs
Anxiety proves groundless
Trust develops

The Fate of the Omnipotence Illusion

The child who works through the devaluation of his omnipotence comes to believe that while he is not omnipotent, his parents are, and he is safe in their care. He proceeds through middle childhood in a protected state, at least until adolescence generates yet another disillusioning experience.

With adolescence the illusion of parental omnipotence goes the same way his first illusion went. As the child matures, particularly in his capacity to think in more complex ways, he begins to see his parents not as the king and queen but as members of a group of persons variously called adults and parents. He begins to see his mother as a mother, and perhaps not necessarily the most competent one on the block. When this insight arrives, the child is forced to re-examine his working comprehension of power.

Many adolescents are disturbed by the knowledge that their parents are not all powerful. It has both attractive and upsetting aspects. It is attractive because it suggests to the child that he or she is going to be free to run their own lives. Their striving for independence is heartened by this knowledge. However, it is upsetting because it leaves them without a protective power base. "If my mother and father are not omnipotent, then my faith in their power to succor me under all circumstances was misplaced. What if something terrible happens? Who now will rescue me?"

To be aware of one's parents' fallibility is to be vulnerable once more. This is one reason adolescents seem so impossibly contrary at times.

If a fifteen-year-old girl asks her mother, "What shall I wear to the dance?" there is no right answer. If Mother replies, "Why don't you wear the pink dress?" the child will say, "Oh, Mother, you're always telling me what to do." If Mother says, "I'm sure whatever you choose will look nice," the child will complain, "Why is it you never help me?"

This is the adolescent situation. One moment they want to be told what to do, and the next no way will they tolerate that kind of ordering about.

There was a time in the history of the world when the adolescent solved this problem by transferring omnipotence from his parents to God, who was then seen as a benign and potent protector. I believe that the phenomenon of adolescent religiosity used to arise, at least in part, out of this psychological sequence.

There is not a widespread personal faith of this dimension among young people today, and so this route to security is not open to most of them.

What then happens to these children? I believe that in most cases something like this goes on. If the child has had good parenting, that is to say reasonable expectations, well enforced, he will have coped with most of the things that come his way. Coping brings confidence. With each growing up task mastered the child feels more competent. Eventually he comes to feel, "I have coped with most things that have come my way, and so I can probably cope with those yet to come."

So it is that the reasonably mature adolescent ventures into the world a bit apprehensive perhaps, but not overwhelmed by his new independence.

However, the child who has not worked through earlier phases of his growth is unlikely to have succeeded enough to build this kind of confidence. He may well find the world overwhelming, and some-times he may search for some omnipotent being to attach himself to.

These days gurus and Messiahs abound, ever ready to absorb new followers, ever ready to make decisions for them, to pander to their needs, be these for the disparagement of the establishment or the assertion of their right to continued and unremitting pleasure. Is this not what Charles Manson had to sell? Self- indulgence without guilt?

If one reads the story of the Manson family, how like omnipo-tent children are these middle-class hedons, these egocentric defiers of conventional morality?

What of the person who reaches adult years and has not worked through his omnipotence devaluation? Do such persons exist? Indeed they do. A successful outcome of omnipotence devaluation is not inevitable, and some persons grow to adulthood having constructed an adaptive pattern that still contains the omnipotence illusion. While this is most often a crippled state of psychological being, it is not incompatible with some kinds of success, for example high achievement in such power-tinged occupations as governing people and directing plays.

Indeed unrestrained omnipotence may be a mental set favorable to certain kinds of creativity, for to believe in one's omnipotence is to be freed from those mental constraints which may hem in humbler men, impressed as they are with the greats who have gone before.

Sigmund Freud was, I believe, a man like this. Listen to this fragment of his childhood. When Sigmund was ten years old, and his sister eight, their mother "who was very musical, got her to practice the piano, but though it was at a certain distance from the cabinet, the sound disturbed the young Freud so much that he insisted on the piano being removed, and removed it was. So, no one in the family received any musical education, any more than Freud's children did later."

Psychoanalyst Eric Fromm, commenting on this incident, says, "It is not hard to visualize the position the ten-year-old boy had acquired with his mother when he could prevent the musical education of his family because he did not like the noise of the music."

This smells mighty like an unresolved omnipotence-devaluation phase to me, as do some other aspects of Dr. Freud's personality.

If one reads the lives of many intensely creative artists, the pattern of unresolved omnipotence often shines through. Perhaps this is why so many of them have been impossible people quite unable to find happiness in life. It is a heavy price to pay for creativity is it not?

So, not all persons work through the omnipotence-devaluation phase of adaptive growth successfully. Some spend their lives fighting the same battle over and over again. Because they have not learned to trust, their security continues to depend on control, control of the persons and events that touch their lives. They battle endlessly to dominate those persons, to determine the course of events. Their marriages reflect this psychopathology. They make terrible parents.

Some such persons move the battleground into the community. They fight the boss or the police. Indeed, many criminals have prominent omnipotent child characteristics. One has only to read their accounts to realize how contemptuous they are of community authority and how much their criminal behavior is intended to prove, "You aren't the boss of me. I don't have to do what you say."

The Attainment of Humility

In the normal case, man's appreciation of the nature and locus of power in his affairs continues to grow throughout his lifetime. Recognizing the facts of power and his own helplessness proceeds at different rates for different persons, but eventually the reality imposes itself on us all. The knowledge of the inevitability of one's own death is a powerful stimulant to this growth.

Death is the ultimate humbling, and fear of it for some persons is more a fear of loss of power than of pain, for to accept one's own death is to acknowledge one's ultimate helplessness.

For the Christian, of course, this acknowledgment is the beginning. The believer is told he must "come as a child," that is "acknowledging his powerless state," if he is to experience his salvation. And others, commenting from a philosophical rather than a religious base, have said similar things. Henry Frederick Amiel tells us that "humanity only begins for man with self-surrender."

Many who have come close to the reality of their own death report that the experience illuminates their lives from then on.

The journey toward a realistic appreciation of the nature of power ends when one comes to grips with and accepts his own mortality. How many reach that goal is in doubt, for the journey requires that a man be brave and honest with himself and others. To face up to this he will need the best adaptive equipment his parents can give him. A successful working through of the omnipotence -devaluation phase of psychological growth is the first and most crucial step towards acquiring that equipment.

The Need for Discipline

It seems obvious that Mother must win some of the battles-of-wills if she is to lead her child through the omnipotence-devaluation phase. She does not have to win them all, but to go on allowing her child to think everything is his idea or charming him into compliance is simply to postpone the inevitable.

Even so, many modern mothers don't see it this way. They have, up to now, been caring for an infant. It is natural for a mother to defer to her infant's demands. It is not only a rational act in view of his helplessness, but also it is an instinctive maternal response. But once the child is on his feet and talking a bit, it should become clear that Mother has another duty to her child besides simply nurturing him. That duty is training him. That training involves discipline, that is *setting limits* and *expecting things* of him.

Maternal awareness of this new need arises naturally. The toddler begins to intrude upon his mother's day. Since he is not napping so much and is on his feet and can follow her around demanding that she play with him, Mother has to begin denying him occasionally. If not, she will become his slave. Self-respecting women are not prepared to do this.

Mother begins to feel he is too big to whine and be so demanding. She begins to recognize that if he continues in his way, others won't make the same allowances for him she is prepared to make. In this natural way, mothers move from simply nurturing the child to training him.

They do not need to read a book to see the need for this transition. Indeed, it might be better if they did not, for many modern child-rearing books overemphasize the nurturant aspects of child rearing. Indeed, some claim that all that is necessary to rear children is unstinting love; the training will take care of itself. Furthermore, by the liberal use of negative examples involving deprived, abandoned, and neglected children, many such books scare mothers away from their natural recognition of the need for discipline and training.

Some mothers become militant in their condemnation of discipline. One such mother, who happened to be dealing with an unusually articulate three year old, was determined to be the best mother this world has ever seen. So, when her three year old questioned every limit and expectation offered, Mother answered her questions, repetitious as these often were.

When I pointed out to her that the child was not really seeking information, she was simply delaying compliance, Mother protested, "Surely the child is entitled to an explanation of why the thing is required of her."

I pointed out to her that the child had had the explanation several times already. I advised Mother thus, "Tell her, 'I told you why yesterday, and we don't need to explain again. Let's get started.'"

Mother then told me that her child would simply not accept this, that she would want a further explanation of Mother's refusal to explain, which she, the mother, would then feel compelled to offer, and so further delay would occur.

"You are the mother," I told her. "You aren't required to answer every question your child puts to you. Just tell her to do it and if she asks why then say, because I am telling you to do it. Now, no more stalling."

Mother was appalled. No way would she ever tell her child to do something simply because "Mother said so." To her mind this was hopelessly authoritarian. That, of course, was the end of me. She went home and returned to her *child rearing is a relationship of equals'* manual.

If parents are to disillusion the child's infantile omnipotence, they must appreciate the true situation between the parent and the pre-school child. In no respect, except in his rights as a human being, is the child equal to the parent. He has almost no knowledge, experience or judgment and is largely unable to understand the real world in which he lives. He cannot deal with his feelings and will follow them straight into serious difficulty if someone doesn't set limits for him. To allow him an equal voice in affairs concerning him, simply because he demands it, is an abdication of the parents' responsibility to be the parents.

Disillusioning the omnipotence of the pre-school child depends upon such a comprehension of parenthood. The fact is the parent is in charge of the bulk of the toddler's life. While the parent does not have to be mean or overbearing, she should make no bones about saying to the child, "No, you can't climb on the window ledge," and take the child down despite his protests.

All children occasionally protest when they can't have their way. Sometimes these difficulties can be minimized with a little tact and wise management. For example, warning the child of an impending change of direction is often helpful. "In five minutes we're going to have supper." The child screams, "No!" But you leave and say nothing. During that five minutes the notion of supper drifts about his mind, and when the five minutes is up and you come for him, he will jump up to accompany you and ask, "What are we having?"

The important thing is that the child ends doing what he is supposed to do when he is supposed to do it. Children learn more from events than they do from words, and if the child regularly does what he should at the time he should, eventually he comes to accept the parents' right to set limits on him. So it is his omnipotence illusion is gradually dispelled.

But what of the child who, despite reasonable tact and consideration, still will not do as he is told and, if one insists, initiates a battle-of-wills and ends having a temper tantrum? If mother is to win the battle of wills and promote his adaptive growth, she will have to cope with the tantrum. How? By dealing with the situation consistently and effectively. Here's my method to do that

Controlling Temper Tantrums

Many parents come to me with pre-school children who are having temper tantrums whenever they cannot have their way. Though many of the mothers are sure there is something terribly wrong, what it usually comes down to is a high energy child in a vibrant but normal omnipotence-devaluation phase which Mother doesn't know how to handle.

Often, before I can outline a program for the control of tantrums, I have to deal with some common misunderstandings. Some persons feel that if the child is having a lot of temper tantrums he or she must be horribly discontent, and the problem is therefore one of nurturance. They feel the child is angry because he is not receiving an adequate amount of affection, that Mother does not love him enough. Most often this is not the case.

To be sure neglected or rejected children will be discontent because of their lack of nurturance, and may express themselves through temper tantrums when things are expected of them. Even so, it is more often the case that such children become sullen and passively contrary. These children need more than better discipline. Their first need is for better nurturance.

Most children having temper tantrums are not, in my experience, in trouble with nurturance. To be sure the mother and child aren't presently experiencing much joy in each other's company, but that is the result of the temper tantrums, not the cause of them. Most such cases in my practice come down to a temperamentally intense child reacting to the psychological pain of omnipotence devaluation with the same vigor he brings to the rest of living.

Once I am sure there is no special cause for the tantrums, I set up a program for their control. Let me illustrate this program with a case. Let's call our willful little three year old Terry.

"He has temper tantrums all the time," the young mother complained. "He throws himself down and he yells and kicks, and he keeps it up until he's hoarse, red in the face and sweating. I try to comfort him, but no way. Once he's started there's no talking to him; I don't think he hears what's being said."

"Have you any idea what triggers these?" I asked her.

"Anything! Any refusal! Cross him in any way and he starts yelling and demanding. I can't always give in to him," the mother said, shaking her head in despair, "But it seems the only way to keep peace. I had no idea the terrible twos could be so terrible; he was such a sunny child up until six months ago."

Terry had always been an energetic and lively child, but a sunny one who was affectionate, approachable and doing fine in his physical and mental development. He walked at a year, he had a few words then, and seemed to have his bowel training almost under control.

But shortly after he turned two, Terry had become very demanding, a little clingy, and the temper outbursts had begun.

For the last four or five months he had been having multiple temper tantrums. Their frequency had increased to the point he was now having as many as ten outbursts in a day. There might have been more if it was not for the fact that Mother *walked on eggs* when she was dealing with him.

As is so often the case, Terry had become more clinging of late and settling him at night had become a problem. "Lie down until I go to sleep" had become his demand, and since he would have a tantrum if he didn't get his way in this, Mother had taken to lying with him until he went to sleep.

I explained to the mother that Terry's tantrums were not caused by emotional deprivation or conflict but were his intense way of reacting to a normal phase of growth. I then explained the omnipotence-devaluation sequence to her.

"The trick is to find a reasonable way to manage the tantrums. Here's my program for dealing with temper tantrums."

TEMPER TANTRUM PROGRAM
The signal
The silent seven
The removal
The timing
Persist

The Signal

"When Terry begins to yell and scream, stand back, point your finger at him, and say, 'You're having a tantrum.' Then cross your arms and look at him."

Mother is to point her finger for two reasons. The first is that small children, like express trains on tracks, need simple signals if they are to grasp the essential information, *en passant* as it were. The second is that the yelling child is often making so much noise he may not hear the accompanying word.

The word doesn't have to be *temper tantrum*. It could be *fuss* or *whoop de doo*. It doesn't matter so long as it always the same word. One Vancouver mother said. "You're Stanley Parking." This was because one day when she and her husband had taken the boy to Stanley Park, he threw such a wing ding that they had to take him home again. Now, when she says 'Stanley Parking,' her child understands exactly what she is talking about.

The signal is just that, a signal. In time it should register with the child and indicate that Program A is up and running.

The Silent Seven

Once the initiating signal has been sent Mother crosses her arms, looks down at her child, and counts to seven. In her head! This is why I call it the *silent seven*. Soon the child realizes that, when Mother's arms are crossed, some kind of timing process is underway.

One four year old whose mother began to use my temper tantrum control program was really impressed with the silent seven, particularly its arm-crossing component. As soon as Mother crossed her arms and began the silent seven he would stop yelling and complain to his mother, "Don't cross your arms." Then he would wander off, tantrum terminated, muttering to himself about weird mothers who were forever crossing their arms.

The purpose of the silent seven is to give the child time to stop his tantrum before removal takes place. Though this will not happen for a while, as the program begins to work, it will become apparent how essential to the training process the silent seven is. Without it there would be no opportunity for the child to improve.

To count out loud is to signal seven times and defeat the program.

The Removal

"In the beginning," I told his mother, "Terry will not stop fussing during the silent seven and it will necessary to remove him." The best way to accomplish removal is to escort, propel or carry the child to the room one plans to use for containment. Since most children will come right back out again, it is necessary to secure the door. I think it best if the door is secured ajar with a long and sturdy hook and eye. This contains the child but it does not separate him to the degree a closed door does. Furthermore, it allows one to place the containment timer outside the door, on the floor, where the child can see it but not reach it. The removal is intended to deal with the tantrum. One cannot stop the child yelling, but one can terminate its communicative import by putting the child in his room.

If other methods of removal will suffice, then they may be used instead. But beware, they might not be effective. For example, one mother said she would prefer to have him go to a corner of the kitchen and sit in the chair for four minutes.

"If he will stay," I agreed.

"I think he will," she said and she was right, but what he did was sit there and harass her for the four minutes. I would have preferred that he got the message, "if you are going to whoop and call names then you can't be out here with me."

Some mothers are concerned about locking the child in his room. In part, I agree. But only in part. Omnipotent children are concerned about separation and putting them in a closed room might generate some separation concern. This is why I prefer the door ajar. It contains him, but it does not separate him.

Removing the child is better than restraining him physically. Restraint remains acutely interpersonal and can quickly accelerate out of bounds. It is better if the child goes to his room and both parent and child have a chance to cool off.

The Timing

There needs to be a containment timer; one of those portable egg timers that ding when the time is up works well. I usually instruct Mother to place it on the floor out of the child's reach but within sight through the door jamb. I recommend it be set for four minutes.

There are two reasons I like to use the visible timer. In the first place, he can't con a timer. It won't go faster because he is woebegone or because he is screaming. But a mother's heart may soften or her resolve weaken and she may let him out. This says to the child that he can control his egress, which does nothing to disillusion his omnipotence.

The second reason I like to use the timer is because it tells the child there is an end to the detention. To put a child in his room for an indefinite period is much more liable to lead to destructive behavior. The child is like a prisoner with a life sentence; why shouldn't he tear the place apart?

"Four minutes is an awfully short time," some mothers say.

"But it is enough to make the action communication that we want to make," I reply. "It says to the child, 'you can't do this, and if you do I will give you a consequence.' On a deeper level it says to the child, 'you are the child and I am the parent. Some things I decide, and this is one of them.' "

I usually take the opportunity to point out to the parent that it isn't the magnitude of the consequence that effects the child's behavior, it is the consistency and inevitability of the response that carries the action communication. "Four minutes regularly applied is enough to do that. Furthermore, since you may have to do it seven or eight times the first day or two, four minutes is long enough. If you make it longer you won't be able to keep it up."

So when Terry has a tantrum, he is taken to his room, kicking and screaming, and is deposited, door latched ajar, with the timer going for four minutes. Of course his indignation knows no bounds.

When the dinger sounds, Mother opens the door. "Your time's up. You can come out now."

Terry does. Like the bull entering the arena. Soon his tantrum is in full flower again.

Mother points her finger at him and says you're having a tantrum. Then she gives him the silent seven, returns him to his room, fixes the latch, sets the timer and retreats to the kitchen. When the four minutes are up, she lets him out.

The whole thing begins again, and she will have to return him again. Once more she follows the routine, giving him the signal and the silent seven before removal.

The fourth time Mother lets him out, gives him the signal and starts the silent seven, Terry will stop yelling.

While I don't know for sure what is going on in such a child's mind, I think something like this is happening. "Migawd! She's doing that bit with the finger and arms again. I know what comes next." So he falls silent and walks off muttering about mean mums and crossed arms.

Persisting

In the usual case the child will go through the whole perform-ance again later the same day. This is all right, for as long as Mother goes through her routine exactly as designed, she is giving Terry his second, third or fourth lesson, and it is through repetition that children learn. The more frequent the repetition, the quicker the learning. The important thing is that each lesson send exactly the same message.

In the usual case it takes two or three days of this kind of training before its effectiveness begins to show. Soon the response is of this order. When Mother takes a step back, points and says in a quiet voice, "Terry, your having a tantrum," fifty percent of the time he will stop during the silent seven, and fifty percent he will have to go to his room. But only for one trip. In a couple of weeks the signal is all that is necessary to stop the tantrum.

This program is very sensitive to its details. Never, for example, repeat the signal before following through. This tells him you don't always mean it. And don't let him con you into letting him out before the time is up.

Secondly, guard your timer. Once the child realizes "It's that timer I can't con," it may disappear into the garbage.

Thirdly, don't let him define tantrum. "I was only kicking not yelling, that's not a tantrum." You're the mother. You decide what is a tantrum and what isn't.

It took three heavy days to convince Terry's mother the program was going to work. When I saw her the next week she was feeling much better about things. "He still has occasional tantrums," she said, "but most times when I back off, point the finger and give him my spiel, he stops fussing before he has to go to his room."

Terry still wants his way, still wants to do what was in his mind to do, but he has learned that when the finger points and the word 'tantrum' is heard in the land, unless he cools it immediately, he will find himself in his room. Seeing no option, Terry now bitches a little but complies with the limit or expectation that triggered his resistance. He comes to supper or gives up on the idea of going to the park "this very minute."

The psychologically crucial event, of course, is that Terry has begun to accept his mother's discipline. He is obeying her and finding that doing so, while sometimes inconvenient, has not the tragic consequence he feared. While he cannot control his mother as he once imagined he could, she still gives him what he needs.

Terry's obedience, however generated, is still obedience. It is incompatible with his omnipotence illusion. Terry's adaptive growth has been well served by this program to control his tantrums.

Such parenting success has a useful effect on mothers too, and often after a program of this kind, one hears mothers say something like the following: "I don't know what got into me, letting that child bully me. I mean, I am the parent, and he is the child."

Having grasped the nettle of discipline, done the hard thing and found it to be within her capacity, Mother develops respect for herself both as a parent and a person. Furthermore, often to her surprise, she discovers her child is not angry with her for being strict; in fact he seems sunnier, and they have begun again to enjoy being together.

When the child is a pre-schooler, a program like this is often all it takes to get adaptive growth in motion again. However, if Mother had not found a way to deal with Terry's tantrums and he had continued on his willful and demanding course, in a few years he would have been well into the omnipotent child syndrome. Then the task would become much more difficult. And once children are into adolescence it becomes almost impossible for parents to alter an inadequate coping style.

For the eight year old having temper tantrums the program often needs to be modified. How modified? He still needs the signal. He still needs some form of silent seven. He still needs containment for a short period of time.

However, removal can be a problem. What if, when mother says go to your room, he slides under the dining room table, gets a scissor lock on one of the table legs and yells, "Gonna make me?" What is mother to do now?

She cannot drag him and she should not try. She should say, "You have one minute to get there or it will cost you," and go away.

"Cost me what," he will call.

Mother should not answer. However, what it will cost him is a punishment card, perhaps no TV after supper that night. He won't go to his room but it will have cost him. After four such episodes and punishments, when mother says you have one minute, he waits thirty seconds then comes out. "OK, I'll go but not because of you. I want to be in my room."

So much then for the omnipotence-devaluation component of adaptive growth. It is time now to discuss the second cardinal characteristic of the syndrome, the child's continuing egocentric perception of the world, so that we can see how its opposite, the capacity to read and accommodate to the needs and rights of others, can be nurtured in the child.

3

EGOCENTRICITY

"Johnny! It's nearly time for supper. Better go wash your hands," Mother called from the livingroom door.

Eight-year-old Johnny, slumped in the big chair, his eyes fixed upon the television, gave no indication of having heard.

"Johnny! In five minutes supper will be served." Mother wiped her hands on her apron and took a step into the room.

Johnny did not flicker an eyelid.

It was nearly time to take the potatoes off the burner. Mother considered leaving him there. But darn it, this was the fourth time that day Johnny had left her dangling when she spoke to him. Mother came part way across the room, raised her voice a decibel or two and called, "Johnny! . . . Did you hear me? I said wash your hands for supper."

Johnny frowned and brushed at his ear as though a fly were buzzing somewhere in the distance.

Mother clumped over, "Johnny! Did you or did you not hear me tell you to wash you hands?" A frown of annoyance crossed Johnny's brow.

Mother placed a heavy hand on Johnny's head, turned his face toward her and snapped, "Johnny Williams. You look at me when I speak to you."

Though Johnny's face now pointed in her direction, his eyes had swiveled to keep the television screen in focus.

Mother turned the chair he was sitting in.

Johnny looked up at her and, shaking his head in exasperation, said, "Do you have to bug me all the time? I heard ya. I was going to do it. Inna minute, inna minute! Gee whiz! Bug! Bug! Bug!"

Mother turned off the television, pointed him toward the downstairs washroom, and retreated to the kitchen. "I suppose I do bug him," she muttered to herself. "But if he'd just answer, I wouldn't have to. If I don't bug, he won't do it. He'd never have washed his hands. He'd just sit there until I fetched him. 'Inna minute, inna minute!' Him and his inna minutes!"

That night after supper, Mother discussed the incident with her husband. "It's as though he were deaf. Maybe we should get his hearing checked?"

You'd be surprised how many parents arriving in my office have first had their child's hearing checked. With negative results. Johnny's problem is not hearing, it's attending. And the problem is not neurological either. It's classical immaturity.

In their hearts, the parents know the child has no trouble hearing. As Johnny's father said later, "Whisper something about going to McDonald's for a milkshake, and he hears from thirty feet away."

The problem has nothing to do with the eardrum or any other part of the acoustic chain. The problem has to do with egocentricity. Much of the time Johnny is immersed in self. He simply doesn't recognize his obligation to respond to others when they speak to him. Like the normal three year old, Johnny comprehends the world as though he were the sun and all others planets orbiting around his being.

All small children are egocentric. It is their natural state and they need to be trained out of their immersion in self. When this training is lacking the child is on the road to an egocentric lifestyle. As Sherwood Anderson, the playwright, put it, Johnny is afflicted with the disease of self.

Johnny's mother has been fostering Johnny's egocentricity by accommodating to him when she should have been requiring him to accommodate to her. Unwittingly she has taught him something she did not wish him to learn.

Johnny has learned that when his mother calls from the living-room door with a message, one of two sequences will follow. Either she will call him twice and go away, or she will call him three times and not go away. In the second case she will approach him, place her hand on his head, swivel his chair or whatever it takes to make sure he gets the message, and deliver it. She will also give him a little static.

Johnny knows there's a better than even chance Mother will give up and go away. Why break his concentration? Why disturb his TV viewing when, with a little bit of luck, he may not have to? Maybe he'll lose a few, but the worst that will happen is that he'll get yelled at.

For Johnny, the system works well. Mother has become his social secretary, screening out the you-can-get-away-with-it calls from the you-must-respond calls.

So long as the parent accommodates to the child in such a fashion, the child will not leave his egocentric cocoon. He will retain that pervasive self-orientation that is so characteristic of the omnipotent child

Manifestations of Egocentricity

Retained egocentricity manifests itself as symptoms in family life; in the community, particularly with peers; and in the moral development of the child.

In Home Life

Parents complain, "Everything has to go his way. If we plan something as a family and he doesn't want to go, he makes a terrible fuss. We can't seem to make him see that others have rights too; that his brother, for example, is really looking forward to going to the park to see the whales. There is no convincing him that perhaps next time the family will be doing something he wants."

All that is in the egocentric child's mind is how his plans are being disrupted by the contemplated action. He is unable to place himself in the point of view of others and see how by doing **his** thing he will interfere with others doing **theirs**.

Furthermore, if the family insists upon him accommodating, as they must do if they are ever going to disillusion his egocentricity, he is resentful. And he lets them know it, often in ways that annoy and disrupt.

"Here's the trouble," Mother says, "if we don't go to see the whales, it's not fair to the rest of us, but if we do, he finds some way to spoil it for everybody. He'll whine or sulk. Perhaps even throw a wingding."

One mother told of an incident which illustrates how imperceptive these children can be. "We were watching TV, my husband, myself, and the two younger ones. At about 7:15 pm Chip came barreling in from play. Well, he just marched straight across the family room, nearly stepping on his little sister in transit and, without so much as a by your leave, changed the channel."

"'We were watching that, Chip!' the kids and I protested. My husband took action. He changed the channel right back again. You should have heard the howls of outrage."

"'But I'll miss my show,' Chip yelled. And he kept yelling. Until my husband marched him upstairs, nobody heard a word from the TV. Eventually he came back down, but he sulked the rest of the night. He still believes he's the injured party. He just doesn't seem to recognize that the rest of the family have rights too."

I'm sure most normal families experience episodes like this. Some call it a phase. With the three-year-old you could call it a phase. But if the phase is to pass, children need to be taught to accommodate to others. Most learn the hard way, that is by occasionally missing their TV program because a clash of rights has arisen. After a few such clashes the normal child begins to take note of the situation of others before seeking to impose their desires on the group. When children fail to show such growth, they are not passing through the phase.

Egocentricity manifests itself in other ways. Consider these common parental complaints.

"You can't discuss anything with him. He hears only himself."

"He never stops to think. I could be standing, burning my fingers on a casserole, and he'll stand right in front of me, demanding that I fix his stuck zipper. Now!"

"When he plays games, the only turn he's interested in is his own. And he's great for changing the rules when it suits him."

"He has no sense of property. If he wants to use something that belongs to somebody else, he just takes it. But take something of his and see what happens!"

"He says whatever comes into his head and never seems to think how his words might offend others. My daughter, who's three years younger, knows better than he does in matters like that."

"He has a fierce sense of justice, but it's one-way justice. All he cares about is what's fair for him, not for others."

All of these behaviors make for tension in family life and, by the time parents come to my office, life at home has often deteriorated to the point that there is very little good will remaining between parent and child.

In the Child's Community

As one might imagine, the child's egocentricity serves him even more poorly outside of his home than in it. Parents may not like his behavior but they do not reject him because of it. Children are less tolerant and egocentricity forms the core of most peer problems.

The usual story is that the child plays poorly. He is happy to play baseball when he's at bat, but when it's his turn to be in the field, he goes home, Or he tries to run the play, wants to change the rules. His bossy self-centeredness alienates his peers who can be very direct. They call him names, ridicule him for his immaturity, and before long he is very much on the edge of the group.

Since the child does not understand how he offends, and is hurt by the rejection he experiences, he reacts. In time he reacts first. He becomes belligerent and quarrelsome. Soon he is starting each day with a chip on his shoulder, and quickly generates the rejection he anticipates.

Sooner or later most such children start withdrawing. They begin going to the library at lunch time or recess rather then remaining on the playground. A common pattern for the egocentric child is to start playing with younger children, those a grade below who, flattered by the attention of the older child, will let him organize the play his way. Besides he is bigger and stronger than grade two kids and can dominate them.

Many egocentric children begin to play with one child only, often one with social difficulties of his own who has to take whomever he can get. The play of these two egocentrics is often painful to behold as each insensitively seeks to impose his agenda on the other.

If a child is to be accepted by his peers, he needs to make some effort to fit in. He needs to stand back a moment, read the action going on, its rules and goals, and take into account the social nuances, such as who's leading and who's following. Then he must find a way to insinuate himself into the social exchange and gain acceptance.

For the normally maturing child this isn't really as complicated as it sounds, but it does take some perceptivity and a capacity to consider the point of view of others. The egocentric child has little of either of these. He reads only his own desires. If the group is playing a game, he'll barrel in and take over the action he finds most attractive, i.e. picking up the bat in a game of scrub baseball. Of course this transgresses the social contract, and he is rejected for his imperceptivity. Since he truly doesn't know what he did wrong, he goes away convinced they are rotten kids who don't like him for no good reason at all.

There are other ways in which the defective social judgment of the egocentric child manifests itself. For example, a three or four year old may throw a stone. Though we scold him for it, we understand that he means no serious harm, he just isn't yet able to comprehend the possible consequences of his action.

On the other hand, we feel the ten year old who throws a stone ought to know better. But if the particular ten year old has remained egocentric, he probably doesn't. Such children know only their own anger and are imperceptive about the possible consequence to their victim.

Such insensitivity is one of the major components of adult criminal behavior. Once I asked an adolescent why he had stolen a car. 'Because I needed to get downtown,' he replied. I asked him if he did not consider that the car belonged to a man who had worked and paid for it. 'But I don't have a car,' he replied, not without indignation, and thought that a sufficient answer.

As children grow older, they grow capable of social decentering, that is, become able to move their locus of perception from themselves to the point of view of another. This temporary shift into the victim's mind would have enabled the child, in the stone-throwing instance, to imagine how it might feel to be the recipient of the stone, such that, when he returned to his own point of view, he might decide to name call instead of throw the stone.

As peer problems continue, the egocentric child is forced to make some kind of a patch-up social adaptation. Certain of these patch-up adaptations lead to further psychological damage.

Playing the class clown is one such adaptation. Boys playing only with the girls is another. Or girls playing exclusively with the boys may be a solution the socially inept child happens upon.

Some of these children become scapegoats. What they have done is develop a special role in the group, that of victim. If one watches them in action it soon becomes clear that they are as much generators of the role as recipients of it.

Occasionally, when this situation becomes intolerable, parents will transfer a child to another school. They hope to give him a fresh start. This may help, especially if others measures to promote his adaptive growth are being taken. However, in many cases, within a month or two, he has slipped into the scapegoat role again.

Other children develop what I call a negative identity. They give up trying to be accepted as a worthwhile person and settle for another role, that of the bad guy, the cut-up, the daring kid who daily goes to the principal's office. They have decided it is better to be notorious than despised. [1]

If the developing child is to be successful with his peers he is going to have to tune in, become aware of other people's rights and needs: in short, become less egocentric. The failure to accomplish this leads to social ineptitude which itself leads to progressive isolation and unhappiness. This is not what parents want for their children.

In Moral Development

A most serious manifestation of continuing egocentricity has to do with the moral development of the child. As children grow older and become more aware and communicative, parents naturally begin to expect them to accommodate to others. They see the child doing things that offend their standards, and they correct him.

"No, Timmy, you have to share your candy."

"That's Sally's toy. Give it back to her."

"That's no way to talk to your grandmother."

In each of these instances it is another person's right that the child is being led to consider. Indirectly, he's being taught not to be so self-centered, to note the impact of his actions on others, and to modify those actions.

1   A negative identity can lead to a particularly difficult life style. Listen to what Mickey McArthur, the notorious Canadian bank robber, has to say about the convict society. "One of the most frequent games the convict plays is I'm More Dangerous Than You Are. He boasts about killing this person, that person, or a whole group of people." Clearly, how bad has become the criteria of worth. I'd Rather Be Wanted than Had, Toronto, Stoddart Publishing Company, 1990.

It is by intruding on the child's egocentricity that parents lead him to become aware that others have rights. While morality may begin with rules, it is perfected by developing such awareness. Let me illustrate what I mean. If I ask the average five year old who comes to my office, "Why shouldn't you steal?" the conversation that follows will run something like this:

"Because it's bad," he responds.

"Why is it bad?"

"Because your mother will get mad."

"Any other reason it's bad?"

"Cause the police'll get you." He starts losing interest in the conversation. However I carry on.

"Why does your mother get mad?"

"Cause it's bad," he says, looking at me as though I were a little dense.

This is all you'll get out of a normal five year old: stealing is bad because Mother disapproves. This is what I call a **rules morality**: behavior is bad because it is against the rules. It is an essential first stage of moral development.

If I ask an eight year old whose adaptive development is proceeding well, why shouldn't you steal? I get a very different answer. What I usually hear is some variant this: "If you take it, they lose it." This morality is not based upon rules but arises from an appreciation of the victim's situation. It is what I call a **social morality.**

The core adaptive capacity involved in replacing the small child's **rules** morality with the older child's **social** morality is becoming less egocentric. The four or five year old has but a vague notion of how his actions affect others; the eight year old is much more capable of social decentering, that is, mentally putting himself in the place of another person and arriving at some comprehension of how his action may affect that other person.

When this growth lags, moral development lags also. For example, there was a thirteen-year-old boy in my community who had, on several occasions, 'borrowed' other children's bicycles without their permission. Eventually the police became involved and made it clear to the boy that this was stealing. This reduced the frequency of the behavior but did not terminate it.

Then one day this boy arrived at the police station on his own. On this occasion he came in the capacity of aggrieved citizen; someone had stolen his bicycle. He was most indignant that he should be victimized in this way.

The police were amused, which infuriated the boy. 'What kind of community was this where the police blithely neglect their clear duty?'

He really thought it wasn't fair. "They chase me when I steal a bike, but when mine gets stolen, they just laugh."

This boy is an egocentric child. He is unable to decenter, that is to shift identity from perpetrator to victim and back again. A more mature child would probably have been embarrassed to seek the help of the police after his prior contacts with them. Not this child; for him the role of perpetrator and victim were totally unrelated life experiences. This is a prominent characteristic of criminals.

Leading the child out of his egocentric posture is crucial to the development of conscience. To be sure, moral training begins with rules, for the child is still too immature to comprehend and appreciate the rights of others. But the goal is that the child become capable of moral understanding, not merely obedience. He must come to feel a sense of *ought*, not merely *must or else*.

To illustrate how parents may begin and further this process, let's take the case of a mother who has decided it is time Megan learns to share. Megan has some candy, so Mother says, "Megan dear, I think you should share your candy with Jane."

Chances are Megan won't agree. Mother will probably ask, "How do you suppose Jane feels watching you eat that candy? Don't you think she must want some?"

Megan, who is a normal three year old, hasn't much idea how Jane feels, and she doesn't much care either. Certainly not when it comes to her candy. She'll most probably respond to mother's questions by clutching her candy to her chest, turning her back and, between hasty mouthfuls, saying, "It's my candy."

What Mother does now is going to have a profound impact on Megan's moral development.

A common error mothers make is to continue talking instead of acting. They make more verbal attempts to have Megan come to an understanding of Jane's state of being. "Can't you see Jane wishes she had some candy?" They lecture not realizing Megan is minimally capable of the social decentering they are expecting of her.

Some mothers will now try to put a guilt trip on a child as yet incapable of feeling guilty. "Not sharing isn't nice, Megan." Or, "You are being selfish."

Though they may scold and disapprove, *they allow Megan to eat all her candy herself.* Megan is not sharing but they don't make her share. 'The candy is her property,' they reason. 'I have no right taking it from her.'

So they deplore but take no action. What does Megan know from deploring?

However, the first step in moral training is to make the correct behavior happen.

In this case, Mother should have taken Megan's candy from her, broken off a piece, given it to Jane, and said "In our house, we share." The crucial thing is to not tolerate the behavior. This means to make the correct behavior happen.

To be sure, the next time Megan has candy she may sneak into her room so that she will not have to share it, but even this is a gain, for it means she is aware of her mother's standard, even if she is doing her best to avoid having to comply with it.

If Megan is made to share regularly, in time she will come to accept this as a rule of the household. The piece of candy she offers may be small, but she will make the offer.

Then one day she will come home from Betty's house and tell her mother, "You know what happened? Betty had some candy and she didn't share! Isn't that awful?" Megan's rules morality is beginning to include the sharing value.

Later, when time and training has led Megan into becoming a less egocentric person, she will be able to convert her rules morality into a social morality. She will be able to perceive Jane's suffering and salivation, intuit her pain, and share out of a dawning sense of humanity rather than a fear of consequence.

Rules morality must precede **social morality.**

Unless the rule is enforced, the social morality cannot develop. Many perfectly moral parents seem not to understand this, and they lecture their children on the wrongness of their acts, but they are too kindly to take the candy from the protesting child and give some to the friend. In such cases, moral development lags.

Similarly with such parents, when the child steals, they are reluctant to confiscate the loot, so they allow the child to keep the item and pay for it later, out of their allowance. Any bank robber would be happy to have a deal like that waiting for him, should he be so unfortunate as to be caught.

When a small child steals the parent must do three things:

1. *Do not allow the child to profit* from the theft.

The child doesn't keep the item and pay for it later; this is profiting.

2. *Make him return the item to the victim.*

This emphasizes the social implication of the stealing behavior by confronting the victim.

3.*Punish the child for stealing.*

Just not profiting is not punishment, nor is the embarrassment of returning the item. Nothing punitive of course. Let him lose his Nintendo for a day or two, or maybe miss one candy day.

If the parent is on the alert for light-fingered behavior and invokes this routine on every such occasion, in time the child will realize the inevitability of Mother's response and learn to forsake the behavior.

The same principles may be applied to the problem of lying. Four and five-year-olds discover lying as readily as they discover mud puddles. Even so, they need to encounter a rule about it if they are ever to succeed to an appreciation of its social content. This is a place where a **jar program** works well. What is a jar program? It is the kind of program with which we are going to handle Johnny's mother-deafness at the end of this chapter. Jar programs are ideal for repetitive little behaviours like 'hitting your sister,' or 'getting down from the table.'

We have seen how egocentricity and morality are at war one with another. The parent who would train his or her child to live a moral life must understand that while rules are the essential beginning, it is leading the child out of his normal egocentricity that completes the job, i.e. leads to a **social morality**.

All children grow older and bigger but they do not all grow up. As a consequence there are many egocentric adults rattling about this troubled society. In these latter times we have seen the emergence of the "me" generation, a pattern of wholly self-oriented young people the worst of whom have multiplied to the point that violence is now endemic, even among elmentary school children.

In order to arm ourselves to prevent such outcomes, let's now examine is detail the normal developmental process that leads the egocentric infant to move from his total "me-ness" to that sensitivity to the needs and rights of others which allows him to accommodate to the world.

Development of Social Decentering

The infant is born egocentric. Since he cannot yet understand where his body ends and the world begins there is no way for him to comprehend himself as a person in an environment of other persons. Technically it will be some time before he can truly be described as self-centered, for he has first to establish a steady sense of self. But when he finally does, it will be as the unwitting center of his limited universe.

Parents tolerate the normal egocentricity of the infant. He is just a baby and one does not expect him to fit into the family; instead one fits the family to him. When he cries Mother tends to his need. The baby cannot explain his problem, but then most mothers don't need an explanation. They can read his cries. These may all sound the same to the father, but most mothers can say with assurance, "He's just hungry," or "He's wet," or "He's just mad, but it's nap time; he'll settle down."

It is not clear to me whether mothers learn to do this, or whether they are, in some mysterious way, psychologically attuned to the child. Sometimes I think the latter. It seems to me that mothers live with the baby for nine months before he has any true reality to others. When he is born he is separated physically from the mother and she from him, but the psychological separation may be much less complete. It is possible there remains a degree of psychological union for the first year, and maybe longer.

In any case, most mothers are sensitive to their infant's needs and respond to them. When the baby cries the mother comes and feeds, comforts or changes him. This of course makes the baby secure, but it does others things too.

In time these needs-arise-and-satisfactions-come sequences teach the baby to discriminate between those unpleasant feelings that are relieved by food and those that respond to some peculiar operation involving cloths and pins. Furthermore, the repetition of these sequences reinforces the child's awareness of the inner feelings that led to his cry and which were alleviated by Mother's response.

However, what if Mother does not respond? What if she does not immediately feed the hungry baby? Perhaps he has to wait while she heats the bottle, or perhaps Mother feels it is time he ate less frequently, so she is going to hold off feeding him for twenty minutes. How does this sequence of need felt, expressed, but satisfaction delayed, affect the child?

It tends to diminish his awareness of his inner distress and increase his awareness of his environment.

Let me explain. At first he will protest vigorously, but, when satisfaction is not immediately forthcoming, his attention turns away from his inner distress to the environment from whence satisfaction comes. So he looks about himself, at first randomly perhaps, but soon he is trying to locate that large, mobile form he has come to associate with warm bottles and dry behinds. He may listen for those sounds of approach whose significance as footfalls is still beyond his comprehension.

Of course, if the bottle arrives immediately, this process of delay, frustration and search is not initiated. So it is that frustration and delay tend to increase the child's awareness of his environment, whereas prompt satisfaction of need reinforces his awareness of his inner self.

From the very beginning, leading a child away from his natural egocentricity, his normal infantile immersion in self, depends upon "intruding" upon him, that is, not accommodating to him in that total fashion appropriate to the care of the newborn.

Mothers have to come to this. It is their natural inclination to respond to the baby's need with prompt satisfaction. When baby cries, Mother jumps. Some mothers are too prompt about this.

I recall a particularly energetic baby who, when his satisfaction was even briefly delayed, let Mother know in terms that roused the neighborhood. His mother, a gentle and sensitive woman, was much pained by his distress. She took to heating his bottle and sitting beside his bed when he was about to wake, ready to pop it into his mouth the moment he first peeped.

When this child grows up, I venture to guess that he will be in good touch with his inner feelings, but his egocentricity is unlikely to have dissipated much. And there's a good chance his omnipotent illusion will remain intact too.

What of the opposite case? What of the child who is raised by the book, fed because it is seven-thirty whether he is hungry or not, or not fed because it isn't seven-thirty yet, regardless of his protests? Let me illustrate this other outcome with a somewhat extreme example.

There is a condition in children called Anorexia Nervosa, a condition in which the child will not eat, seems not to experience hunger, and in some strange way has an unrealistic and intense investment in being slim. Some of these children starve themselves to death.

I had occasion to treat one such child in hospital, a twelve-year-old girl who was a talented television actress. It was necessary to hospitalize her to maintain a level of nutrition compatible with life. In hospital, as at home, she struggled valiantly to avoid food intake and to dissipate calories.

She came to me one day shortly after she'd arrived on the ward and said, "You're going to make me hungry at five o'clock."

"How can that be?" I asked.

"Because that's when you serve supper," she answered.

I was mystified. One is not hungry at five o'clock because five o'clock is supper time; one is hungry because one feels hungry.

In time it became clear to me that this girl had suppressed her inner awareness of the signals we experience as hunger.

In time I realized this was not the only aspect of inner awareness the child had suppressed. She was minimally aware of her emotions. This was particularly evident with anger. She would walk about the ward exuding hostility. Ask her what she was mad about, and she would reply that she was not mad. It took a while, but eventually we realized she really had no awareness of the anger within her.

When I finally put together a picture of her infant care, I saw that her mother, a very egocentric and rigid person, had raised her infant in accordance with an inflexible schedule which was almost totally unresponsive to signs of distress from her child.

In the previous example the mother had accommodated too promptly by sitting beside her infant's crib with the heated bottle; in this instance the mother had accommodated not at all.

Perhaps there was a time when this little girl cried for her bottle because she was feeling hungry, but the bottle's eventual arrival bore no relationship to that experience of hunger. Since these inner signals were irrelevant to satisfaction, in time the child learned to ignore them.

When an internal feeling is responded to, one's awareness of that feeling increases, but when it is not responded to, one gradually extinguishes that awareness. Since the child's other feelings had also been ignored by her egocentric and insensitive mother the child had gradually learned to suppress awareness of them too. By the time she came into my care, she was so out of touch with her feelings that she could accuse me of generating hunger by serving supper at a given time on the clock.

It follows that, if the infant's egocentricity is to be successfully dissipated, he needs to experience a balance between gratification of his needs from an environment reasonably responsive to him, and demands from that environment that he begin to read its content and respond to it. In infancy need-gratification naturally dominates, but increasingly training enters the picture.

The normal two yearold sees the world almost entirely from the perspective of self. Even many three year olds. Here's an example. When my three year old used to join us playing hide and seek, he would stand in the corner, cover his eyes, and giggle merrily, firmly of the belief that if he could not see us, we could not see him.

I don't think we not sure if we fostered his development much by going along with him, but that's what we did. Now his picture is on the dust jacket of this book. It's his wedding day. You will notice that, despite the occasion, his eyes are open.

For the egocentric toddler, events are conspiring to force the issue. Since the child no longer naps mornings and afternoons and is on his feet and can follow Mother around, he is much more into her day. If she is to get anything done, she is going to have to start saying, "No, Johnny, I can't play with you now, I have things to do."

Furthermore, Mother may now have another infant, another egocentric sun about which she is required to orbit. I do not believe the astronomers have yet discovered a planet that succeeds in orbiting about two suns simultaneously, so if Mother is not to fly apart, one of these suns is going to have to become a planet.

Johnny does not like becoming a planet. He prefers being the sun, and he protests his demotion. He may even come up with a solution to the problem. "Let's send the baby back."

Even if a baby isn't involved, the child will still protest his demotion from sun to planet. If he happens to be a particularly intense and energetic child, his protest will be vigorous. If his mother tends to lack assertiveness and to have read a lot of 'love- is- all' child-rearing literature, she may have some difficulty dealing with her insistent toddler.

The more demanding the child becomes, the harder it is to feel loving towards him. Before long Mother begins to feel a little guilty. She begins to wonder if the reason he is cranky is because she is not giving him enough love. In an effort to correct this she accedes to his demands; she stops what she is doing and plays with him. This of course only teaches Johnny that if he just yells long enough, Mother will go back to treat treating him like the sun. It is from such minimal beginnings that problems with continuing egocentricity arise.

On the other hand, if Mother is a self-respecting individual she says to herself, "I'm a person too; it won't kill him to wait a little. It's time he learned." So she tells Johnny, "No, I'll play with you later." She sticks to her guns, putting him in his room if he has a tantrum.

When such happens, Johnny is made to accommodate to her. He has taken the first step on the long journey that will eventually leads him out of normal egocentricity into an increasing awareness of others and their rights.

Until the child is able to recognize that others have their rights and needs and that their intentions may be different from his own, he will misunderstand events. For example, some children think their parents discipline them because parents enjoy the process. The child who turns dressing in the morning into a chasing game is often convinced his mother is having as much fun as he is. It is not until the child has become less egocentric than he can understand his parents' behavior in consistently realistic terms.

I once saw an eleven-year-old girl who told me,"My mother cries to make me feel bad." While some mothers will do this, I happen to know that this mother cried because she was genuinely despairing about her relationship to her daughter. However, her egocentric child interpreted all the world's actions in terms of their effects upon her. "If it makes me feel bad, that must be the reason she did it."

When the child becomes less egocentric and aware of his parent's feelings, he will behave to please the parent instead of to avoid a consequence. Then child rearing becomes a much more pleasant process. Unfortunately, behaving to please does not become a significant mode of action until a considerable amount of adaptive growth has already been achieved.

For the child to be willing to modify his behavior to please his parent, two things are necessary. First, the child must be able to perceive how the parent feels, that is whether she is pleased or displeased. Then the child must be able to comprehend a connection between that parental feeling and his behavior.

The very young child, or an older one who remains egocentric, does not appreciate how his parent feels. All that fills his mind is how he feels. He is being asked to do something he doesn't want to do, or not do something he wants, and frustration dominates his awareness. Clearly the child who is insensitive to his parents' state of feeling will certainly not be moved to modify his behavior on account of a distress he does not comprehend exists.

Even if the child does detect that his parent is displeased or unhappy, he must see a connection between that parent's state of feeling and his behavior. But egocentric children tend to interpret events in terms of how they affect themselves, not others.

To lead the child out of egocentricity, one uses approaches that intrude upon the small child's egocentricity until it dawns on him there are others in the world with other points of view, other desires than those which fill him. This dawning awareness opens the door to training techniques that are less action oriented, more interpersonal and rational. In time, approval-disapproval comes to have sufficient meaning for the child to become an instrument of further training.

Let's return now to a practical example of how parents may intrude upon the egocentricity of their omnipotent child. Let me use the problem with which I opened this chapter. You remember Johnny who did not hear his mother when she called him for supper? Egocentricity is what is involved here. And it's probably showing up in a lot of other places too.

Johnny is immersed in self. He's forever doing his thing. He does not want to be intruded upon. "Inna minute ... inna minute," he says, whether the instruction be "Come for supper," "Hang up your coat," or "Come in the house." Mother can't find a way to move him short of six tellings and a yelling, and she is certainly tired of that.

Here is my program for dealing with the *six tellings and a yelling situation.*

The Second Telling Jar

Mother gets a glass jar and three 'counters': chips, buttons, pearls, whatever's handy in her household. Then, even though what she says probably won't get past the eardrum, to be fair, she explains the program to the child.

"You don't like me nagging and yelling at you whenever I want you to do something, and believe me, I don't like doing it either. So! No more six tellings and a yelling! Here's the new deal. When I want you to come to supper, or maybe other things, I'm going to call out to you: 'Johnny, come to supper, and it's four minutes to second telling.'"

"Four minutes to what?"

"Second telling! And in four minutes I'm going to call to you again with that one phrase 'Second Telling.' That means you have ten seconds to show up on my horizon. If you don't show I'll come fetch you, turn off the TV, and lead you to the table. Whatever it takes. But if I have to fetch you, you will get a chip in your second telling jar."

No answer! The subject does not enthrall him.

"And when you get three chips, you'll get a punishment, like maybe losing one of your TV programs or your bike for a day. Then I remove the chips and we start over again. Every three chips, a punishment."

By now his eyes are glazing over; he's heard this kind of thing before. Never mind. After nine chips and three punishments he'll have figured out how the program works.

The following is the way things usually go. When he doesn't come to supper, or take out the garbage, or get started on his homework, Mother goes through her routine.

Of course the second telling doesn't yet get him moving and Mother has to fetch him to the task. She gives him a chip. He shrugs. Or perhaps he has a tantrum, which she manages with her tantrum control program. She then returns to the subject at hand, the second telling program.

Soon he has earned his third chip and his first punishment. "I don't care. I wasn't planning to ride my bike after school today." This maneuver is called the 'sweet lemon'; all children come into the world equipped to use it. We shall elaborate upon it later when we discuss how to punish fairly but firmly.

Soon Johnny has earned another three chips and another punishment. He may have moved on the second telling once or perhaps even twice, but by no means is the problem solved. Even so, six tellings and a yelling have stopped. Both the household tension and the decibels have been significantly reduced.

Next thing you know he's responding to the second telling call with the cry of, "No sweat. I've only got one chip in the jar." Which means, of course, that he's beginning to keep count. Soon when you call second telling, he comes slumping to the task.

The indicator of progress is that it's now taking him two days to get three chips, whereas the first week he was getting nine chips and three punishments a day.

The second telling program is among the most popular of the specific measures I recommend to parents in trouble promoting the adaptive growth of their child. This is because Mother no longer has to escalate to yelling to get him moving. It's the quiet she finds so refreshing.[2]

2   Even so, not all 'experts' approve of my second telling program. One editor of a woman's magazine declared it was silly and unnecessary. All Mother had to say to the child was, "Come to supper or you won't get any." So he doesn't come. After three nights with no supper, guess who weakens? And isn't sending the child to bed hungry a mean punishment?

The second telling program is what I call a Jar program. There are behaviours that occur frequently, that need systematic correction which of course involves a consequence as a reinforcer. By using a jar, we are able to apply one\third of a punishment to each single offense, and do it now, when it needs doing.

Here is the Second Telling Program in tabular form.

THE SECOND TELLING JAR
Come to supper
Four minutes to second telling
Second Telling
Fetch
Chip in the jar
Three chips = One P Card
Start again

Why is the second telling program so effective? Because it is constructed from the elements of sound discipline. While these will be dealt with at length at a later point in this book it is not amiss to introduce them at this point.

The Elements of Discipline

There are four such elements, the expectation, the time limit, the supervision and the consequence. Let's examine those elements one by one.

The Expectation

The parent must give the child a clear expectation. Nothing vague or advisory such as, "I wish you would take the garbage out now and again, Michael." If he's a witty kid he may reply, "Wish away!" Make it simple, but make it clear it's a *you must*.

The Time Limit

If one does not set time limits, one ends nagging. "Four minutes to second telling," is a time limit. Not only does this take the place of nagging but it also gives the child transition time. Nobody wants to drop what he or she is doing this instant and come to supper or go hang up his coat. The four minutes gives the child time to adjust his mind to the task to come, time to accept the expectation. Soon 'second telling' becomes a magic phrase which moves the child. Indeed it is often the case he soon comes to beat the clock, arriving in the kitchen before Mother has got around to calling out 'second telling' and asking, "Hey, Mom, what's for supper?"

The Supervision

Johnny must come to the task or he is not accommodating to Mother's agenda; she is accommodating to his. This of course panders to his egocentricity and generates no growth. If he does not come on second telling, he must be fetched. Make the behavior happen!

The Punishment

In the case of second telling, the three chips are a method of punishment. If, however, you set up a regular program of getting dressed in the morning and the child does not make it on time, a chip is not enough, He needs a whole punishment such as lose an hour prime time TV, or no bike after school that day.

Why use chips for second telling? Because, if you gave him a punishment for every second telling, he would soon have no privileges left. The main advantage of the chip jar is that it offers a way to respond consistently to a frequently occurring, minor behavioral failure without swamping the child.

It is important that children come to connect the imposed consequence with the behavior that led to it, if they are to change the behavior. The chip is something to give the child **now** that establishes that connection, even though the final consequence does not actually happen until **later**.

Chips are much more than a gimmick. They are a valuable action- communication device. Those who derogate them as childish probably haven't had much experience communicating with children.

These then are the principles of discipline involved in the second telling, and most other disciplinary programs. When each principle is given proper weight in the design of discipline, growth results. Overlook any one of them and the program will fail.

Through the device of 'second telling,' we have intruded upon Johnny's egocentricity. We have invested the outer world with psychological significance. We have directed his gaze outwards and altered his egocentric posture a modicum.

Effective discipline intrudes upon the child's egocentricity.

Furthermore, whenever we require the child to accommodate to us, we also make an action statement about power, letting Johnny know that he is not the boss of the world, that he has, in some things, to defer to his parents' choices. So omnipotence devaluation is also involved.

Finally ,this same disciplinary technique influences the development of the third adaptive competency we are interested in, i.e. "tolerance for normal unpleasure," the subject of our next chapter.

4

PATIENCE AND SELF-CONTROL

The infant is a 'now' creature. When the baby is hungry he wants the bottle, and he wants it **now**. When he's frightened he wants to be made safe by Mother's arrival on the scene. **Now!** When the toddler sees his dessert, no more meat and potatoes for him. Cleaning his room is a mountain of unpleasure to the seven year old who has remained a now creature.

Of course the infant has little or no tolerance for normal unpleasures. This is a capacity that must be developed through practice. How do you practice tolerating unpleasure? By experiencing regular amounts, not so small as not to stretch one's capacity, not so great as to overwhelm it. The omnipotent child has not experienced this steady training and he fails to develop the patience and persistence necessary to cope with the four major unpleasures natural to the human condition ; anxiety, anger, disappointment and tedium.

Let's begin our description of this cardinal characteristic with an example. Here is a common mother-child scenario. It involves getting dressed in the morning. Many mothers of eight- or nine-year-old boys paint the following picture for me.

The Toast and Tears Scenario

"It's twenty to eight, Bryan," Mother calls from his doorway, an ear cocked down the stairwell listening for signs of disaster from the kitchen. "I've got to go back downstairs to look after your little brother. You get dressed now. No dawdling! Remember what happened yesterday?"

Bryan's eyes are open, but there is doubt that his optical cortex is registering visual impressions. He does not answer.

"Bryan!"

He turns his head in the general direction of the sound.

"Bryan? Did you hear me?"

Bryan nods.

"Say something so I know you're really awake."

Bryan grunts.

"No dawdling." Mother whirls and departs, the aroma of burnt toast lending wings to her feet.

Bryan picks up a sock, slowly rolls it, and places the open end over the toes of his left foot. He grabs either side of the sock band and starts pulling. The sock slides over his foot until it reaches the heel. It stops. Bryan gives it a tug. The sock resists. He gives it a dirty look and a mighty tug. The sock does not move from the heel. The inertia of Bryan's effort collapses him backwards across the bed. He lies there, defeated.

As he rests Bryan stares at the water mark on the ceiling. "Looks a bit like Darth Vader." He cocks his head to one side, "Or maybe Jaws, coming in for the kill." He drifts into a fantasy, a mental state infinitely preferable to battling uncooperative socks.

Ten minutes later Mother arrives on the scene. She finds Bryan flat on his back one sock half on, but otherwise as undressed as when she left.

"Bryan! You haven't even started dressing."

Bryan raises his foot in limp denial. "The sock stuck."

"All you have to do is give it a hard tug." Mother pulls him from his lying position on the bed.

"I did."

"Some pairs are a little tight; they stick at the heel. You have to pull really hard." Mother drops to her knees and starts pulling the sock over Bryan's heel.

"I can't pull that hard," Bryan complains.

"If it was after school and you were going over to Jimmy's to play, you'd be able to pull that hard." Mother shoves the sock up his calf.

Bryan says nothing. The fact is he wouldn't have worn socks if he was going out to play. She only checks in the morning.

Mom finishes the job and gets to her feet. "Now get dressed. And hurry or you'll be late for school."

"I wasn't yesterday," Bryan mutters.

"Because I drove you," Mother snaps, getting to her feet. "No way am I driving you today. Finish dressing. No more dawdling." She stomps down the stairs, thumping her displeasure.

Bryan starts in bravely, but the shirt buttons manage to get into holes one step removed from where they ought to be. The thought of undoing each and doing it up again is a mountain of tedium. Bryan turns from that dread prospect and drifts to the window to see what the birds are up to. Nothing much. Soon he's flat on the bed again, sliding off into outer space. That is where his mother finds him ten minutes later when she returns to check on his progress.

"Migawd Bryan. You're not dressed. What's the trouble this time ?"

"The buttons got in the wrong holes."

"Well, take them out and put them in the right holes." Mother again drops to her knees and starts doing it for him. All the while she is lecturing him of the twin subjects of childhood independence and task persistence. "Now," she says as she finishes, "no more dawdling. There's barely time for breakfast as it is." And she leaves.

Bryan returns to dressing. Does pretty well too until he can't find his other shoe. He looks under the bed. It isn't there. Since he happens to be near the bed, and a little discouraged, he drops down for a rest, and that is where Mother finds him seven minutes later.

Now, you must understand, Mother has read all the child-rearing books. She's been through the *natural consequences* bit. She knows Bryan isn't lazy, merely *effort-challenged*. And she believes childhood should be a golden time. Despite all this, and knowing yelling is not an approved form of parent-child communication, she yells. She knows empty threats undermine her authority, but she makes them anyway.

She yells and she threatens. What's more, it works. Bryan scurries about, an eye over his shoulder observing the storm front. Somehow he finds the energy to wash his face, brush his teeth, and comb his hair. It is her standing there emitting thunder and lightning that keeps him on task.

On the way to the kitchen Mother continues to let Bryan know she is not pleased. In fact she uses some terminology she is going to regret later. Bryan ends in tears. There is no time for breakfast so it's out the door with a cold piece of toast in his hand and tears on his cheek.

As she stands behind the window curtain watching him go, Mother is filled with pain and remorse. "Listen to me! Every morning, nagging and tears." She shakes her head in despair. "What a way to start a school day!" She slumps for the kitchen, despairing of her motherhood, ready to turn in her apron and take the night flight to Peru. 1

That afternoon, after flagellating herself all morning, she bakes him a cake to make it up to him. Which he eats happily. However, the next morning, when the sock sticks, the tears and toast scenario is rerun one more time.

The problem is that Bryan tolerance for unpleasure has not stretched. There are several forms of unpleasure. Lets deal with them one at a time.

1   For a further elucidation of the Night Flight to Peru Syndrome the interested reader is referred to my play "Don't Shoot, I'm Your Mother." Vancouver: Palmer Press. 1988.

The Four Principal Unpleasures

There are four types of unpleasure the child encounters and needs to develpo tolerance for. These are tedium, anxiety, disappointment and anger. Let's deal with them one at a time.

Tedium

Tolerating the tedium of tasks that are not much fun is high on the list of childhood unpleasures. "Borrrrring" is the tip-off word.

Tolerating tedium is what is involved in the get-dressed in the morning scenario just described. Whe the child lacks a normal degree of tolerance for his years, it is probably the case that his adaptive growth is lagging.

Bryan has very little tolerance for tedium, in this case that of getting dressed in the morning. Sure the sock sticks, but that is a little fence to climb. Even so, unless he's got a heavy deadline or a wild satisfaction imminent, Bryan just can't climb those little fences. It's the same with his school work; the first number fact he can't remember and he's staring into space. Send him to the basement to get a jar of preserves, and fifteen minutes later he's standing by the work bench having forgotten why he went downstairs.

Bryan's mind is like a car with a worn-out gearbox. The first time it encounters even the most gentle of uphill grades it slips into Pleasure Idle so smoothly that even Bryan doesn't realize forward movement has ceased. So, unless he's constantly supervised, the routine tasks don't get done. Any activity Bryan does not find continuously pleasing he labels **borrrring** and thinks it should not be put on him.

Adaptively immature children are chronically discontent. They feel that unless life is presently joyful they are being short changed. And, if the mother involved is one of those who believes childhood should be nothing but golden every moment of every day, she will undoubtedly take the blame for her failure to make it so.

Because such children are not trained to tolerate tedium, they want everything now. Bryan has remained a 'now' child. Books take too long to get to the good parts, so he reads the comics. He decides he wants to play the guitar, but when he isn't a rock star in two weeks, he quits. It's the same with baseball and hockey; whenever he encounters the need for some practice, whenever he needs to tolerate a little present tedium for some future pleasure, he packs it in with face-saving contempt. "Aw! Baseball's dumb."

There are other forms of unpleasure for which children need to develop tolerance, Let's move on to the second of these.

Anxiety

There are those who feel that childhood ought to be a time free from anxiety. This cannot be. Childhood is a time of steadily widening horizons. Life continuously presents new challenges to the growing child. Each of these is an occasion for anxiety as well as an occasion for growth.

All children have to make a first visit to the barber, to the dentist, to the doctor, perhaps for a shot. They all have to take their first trip down the playground slide or into the swimming pool. Each mastery increases the capacity for future coping with anxiety . Eventually the child can try out for baseball, stand up to a bully, or make a speech in front of the class.

It is important that children be led to cope with such normal fears. The protective parent, who shelters the child too much, robs him of such mastery and delays the process of adaptive growth. This has happened to the omnipotent child. Despite his braggadocio, Dewey is a lot more anxious than strangers know.

Since the sheltered child does not learn to cope with anxiety, he develops techniques for avoiding it. Faced with some new expectation many little children will show their dismay, and the sensitive parent, not wanting to cause him pain, may withdraw the expectation. "All right," mother says to her play school child. "I'll stay with you one more day."

If mother does a lot of this, the child doesn't stretch his tolerance for anxiety, and further he may learn to turn on the woebegones whenever he thinks he needs them. Though sensitive mothers may suspect they are being, they tend to weaken. "OK, I'll lay down with you. But just this once."

Anxiety is an abdominal displeasure, and it can be hard to tell if he's got pain or just the pre-school flutters. If mother errs on the side of playing safe, playschool absences can build up to the point that a school-phobia may be in the offing.

In time such children learn to avoid expectations rather than cope with them. But to avoid all conditions that generate anxiety is to avoid life itself. This happens more than most people think. It is estimated that there are thousands upon thousands of *agoraphobics* populating our cities. These persons, afraid to venture from the safety of their homes into streets and department stores, are really imprisoned in their childhood dependency.

Further, we have finally learned these avoidant adults cannot be analyzed out of their phobias; they need to be taken by the hand and led through the coping they should have experienced as children, the coping that leads to mastery and self-confidence. How much better to do it first time round!

There is a form of anxiety which bears a special relationship to omnipotence devaluation. This is called separation anxiety and it often first observed in relation to this phase of adaptive growth. Early manifestations occur at bedtime, when the three year old wants Mother to lay down with him until he goes to sleep, or cries when the sitter comes, or when he has to be left at nursery school. The child is still fearful of functioning out of the protection of home and parents. It is the author's view that school phobia and agoraphobia are symptoms which grow out of the failure to work through normal separation anxiety when it first arises during the omnipotence-devaluation phase of adaptive growth.

Helping the child to cope with this anxiety is the first major step taken on the long road that begins in tearful panic, softens to apprehensive timidity, slides into lip-trembling bravery, and ends in confident adventurism.

Disappointment

Childhood contains another unpleasure the child needs to master, the unpleasure of disappointment or loss. The six year old, happily anticipating a trip to the zoo, is dismayed when the car comes up with a flat tire. He cries. When he is more mature he manages his disappointment better.

Not so the omnipotent child. He comes apart when the stress is minimal. "You promised," he wails. "You gotta keep your promise. You just go get that flat fixed this minute." And when Mother cannot, or will not, he goes on to a full-scale temper tantrum.

Of course, parents should keep their promises whenever possible, but times of disappointment are inevitable. The child grows from disappointments experienced and mastered. Gradually he comes to handle such unpleasure with increasing self-control.

However, the child will not learn to handle disappointment if he is forever protected from it, and some parents go to great lengths to protect their child from life's little blows. If he loses his dollar, Dad gives him another one. If Mother buys a sweater for Jane, because she needs one and they are on sale, she feels compelled to buy something for Johnny too, so he won't be disappointed. If Bryan's TV plans conflict with his mother's, guess who gives up her show?

For mothers to defer to small children is as natural as to bear them. Less natural, but equally important, is for Mother to recognize when to move away from her infant-centered existence to one in which the child is required to wait a little, to do a mite of accommodating. As she does so, coping begins to take precedence over indulgence, training over nurturance.

There is a particular situation in which parents commonly try to preserve children from disappointment. It has to do with losing pets. If one lives in the city and has a dog or cat, there is a statistical probability the pet will be killed in an accident. Sad, but reality. This is a blow to the child. Understandably, parents try to protect their child from this *trauma.*

What they do is rush out and replace the pet with another. This is the wrong thing to do. Not only does it fail to replace the lost pet, but also it confuses the child. Sometimes it generates conflicts involving loyalty to the old pet and attraction to the new. Most importantly, it interferes with the normal psychological process involved in accepting and coping with loss. The child who loses his pet experiences loss and the kind of unhappiness associated with loss which we call sadness.

Of course the child cries, and the parent comforts him as best she or he can. As time passes the loss is felt less keenly, the hurt heals. This is the normal psychological process involved in dealing with loss, the same adults go through when they lose something precious to them. The child is capable of going through that process, and when he succeeds in doing so, an important thing happens: the child experiences loss and masters it.

To master unpleasure is to increase one's tolerance for the it. Five inches of tedium today seems unbearable, but tomorrow a foot is child's play. Three ounces of anxiety today amounts to terror, but one pound tomorrow is experienced as moderate nervousness. Disappointment that seems unbearable today is barely cause for a "that's life" shrug tomorrow. Like weight lifting, each repetition strengthens the psychological muscle. So it is, as the child experiences his disappointment, he gradually recovers from his sense of loss and is happy again.

The child who loses his cat learns, in the only way such learning takes place, that loss is not inconsolable, that a day will come when he will feel better again. So he is braver, more willing to invest of himself, to care and not fear losing that for which he has learned to care.

There are people who live narrow lives because they are fearful of losing. They will not invest of themselves. They withdraw into their shells like timid snails. For them life is a waiting room for death.

The child who has lost something important while yet a child and survived that loss, becomes stronger, more willing to face future risks. To be brave is to be armed for life.

Anger

There is a fourth unpleasure we all have to master: the unpleasure of anger. Anger is an unpleasant feeling, not only for the object of the anger but also for the angry person. It upsets; it jangles; it lingers. But anger is inevitable, not only in the life of the adult, but also in the life of the child.

The frustrated infant experiences rage. If he had the power to express that rage, it is unlikely any mother would survive the first year of child rearing. He cannot kill, so he screams his rage. By degrees the child, required to do so, will modify his expression of rage such that it becomes vocal anger, then protest, then complaint and finally a dirty look followed by compliance.

Why do people get so upset about dirty looks from kids? Would they rather see a little Lord Fauntleroy smile masking vengeful fantasy?

Anger is an honest emotion. Kids are allowed to feel it. What we want them to do is find some acceptable way to express it. Heree is what I used to say to my kids when they gave me a dirty look. "Think softer, I almost heard that." If they weren't too mad to begin with, they'd end smothering a giggle.

It is characteristic of the omnipotent child that he cannot handle his anger in a fashion appropriate to his years. He is explosive; he has temper tantrums. He goes too far. He says, "I'll kill you," when he is merely unhappy with your behavior. He is abusive when he is simply at odds with your point of view. He threatens. He over-reacts in a way that raises the hackles. He is arrogant and overbearing when disagreement is all the situation calls for. When frustrated, he may hit or throw things or become destructive. It isn't that his frustration is any more acute than other children's but that he cannot modulate his expression of feelings.

Violence in children has become distressingly common these days and newspaper columnist have blamed everything from TV to the devil. Most violent children are grossly immature. Indeed, the three aspects of adaptive immaturity come together in such children, continuing willful omnipotence, egocentricity of such magnitude that they fail to perceive the humanity of their target, and infantile self control when it comes to dealing with the unpleasure of anger. Only a few of these children are truly psychopathic. Most of them are merely infantile.

It is evident that the temper tantrum control program outlined in Chapter Two, as well as disillusioning the omnipotence of the child, play an important part in stretching the child's tolerance for the unpleasure of anger.

In order to illustrate this process further let me describe another technique for managing a lesser manifestation of anger parents often complain about. The behavior in this instance is rudeness.

I hear complaints of this nature. "When he gets mad, he calls me Dumbo," one mother said. "If he gets mad enough he tells me to shut up," another says. "The other day he gave me the finger," a third reports. Don't knock it. Someday he may grow up to be a Prime Minster.

Such gems as "ya gonna make me," or "nyah, nyah, I don't have to do as you say," raise the hackles of parents.

Rudeness is pretty small potatoes if, at the same time, the child is throwing intermittent tantrums during which he kicks his mother and throws things.

First things first! Forget the rudeness until one has the tantrums under control. Then come back to the rudeness.

Supposing mother has eradicated tantrums and is now at this at the point she isn't preapred top tolerate his rudeness anymore. What does she do? She sets up a Rude Jar Program.

The Rude Jar

The Rude jar is simply a jar bearing this label. Mother shows her boy the jar and explains, "Johnny, you are sometimes very rude. You say things like 'shut up' or 'make me' and sometimes you put your finger up in the air like Trudeau."

"Who's Trudeau?"

"A man who should have known better."

"I guess him mom didn't teach him, eh?"

"Never mind his mother. Listen to yours. I don't want you being rude anymore, and I'm going to train you not to be. Here's how it works. Whenever you say or do something rude, I'm going to say *that's rude* and put a chip in the jar."

"Big deal," Johnny snorts. "Chips in the jar!"

"And when you get three chips, you get a punishment."

"What punishment?"

"I'll see. Something like miss *Cops* tomorrow night, or grounding your bike for a day."

Johnny shrugs and departs. 'Another dumb program. It won't last a week,' he thinks.

Johnny will probably get three chips a couple of times the first day, a total of six chips which translates to two punishments. Maybe, if he's an enthusiastic practitioner of the rude art, he'll get nine. That means he gets three punishments. He'll be a bit surprised when Mother follows through the third time but he'll pretend he doesn't care.

The next morning Johnny will get three chips by noon. "What's all this Mickey Mouse about chips?" he will protest, but that afternoon, after two more chips have found their way into his jar, he will clean up his act, maybe even get through the rest of the day with nothing more than the occasional inaudible mutter passing his lips.

The next morning he gets a fast chip, a punishment, and then two more not-quite-so-fast chips. A few hours of verbal restraint then follow. In a few days, he is down to three chips a day and we are getting restraint on fifty percent of the occasions that, in the past, would have resulted in rude behavior.

Of course it is not always that easy. What about the child who says "Dumbo," gets a rude chip, then says, "Dumbo! Dumbo! Dumbo!" You can't keep flinging in chips. What do you do then? The second "Dumbo" you say, "You're out of control," (which is a special form of tantrum), and it's off to his room for four minutes. Soon he is stopping at the first Dumbo chip.

Once he is getting fewer chips, he is restraining himself on some occasions. His mouth opens and closes again before the rudeness emerges. This is enough restraint to generate some self control. This is what we were shooting for, training him to limit his expressions of anger and annoyance to a vocabulary acceptable for his age and situation.

But more than getting rid of rudeness has been accomplished. By teaching him to curb his tongue Mother has stretched his tolerance for the unpleasure of anger. And it is often the case that when the child learns to tolerate more anger without giving way to its expression, he also shows a little more patience, handles disappointment better shows a little more persistence.

Tolerance for unpleasure is a general capacity and what stretches it in one area, stretches it in another. Though the measure might seem small, the adaptive consequence for the passage to adulthood may be large.

We have seen that the normal child who receives effective train training gradually masters the unpleasures of tedium, anxiety, disappointment and anger. The omnipotent child lags in this aspect of adaptive growth as well as the others. He is in danger of becoming a pleasure-bound, pain-avoidant adult.

There are many adults these days who are adaptively immature when it comes to dealing with life's unpleasures. I speak of impulsive, short-tempered persons, who marry in haste but cannot sustain the giving required in the mutuality of marriage. Such persons take the cash and let the credit go; they end up not paying their taxes or get in trouble with their credit card. Since they cannot work well, and resent the boss's authority, and are unrestrained in their expression of this resentment, they tend to drift from job to job. As adults they have grown big, but they haven't grown up.

The worst of these assault and mutilate their fellow citizens. Lacking the self-control to cope with society, they become half humans and end imprisoned to protect society from them.

Listen to how one bank robber describes convicts. "The convict is like a sprinter primed to explode out of the starting blocks at the first crack of the pistol~directly into a concrete wall he fails to see ten feet in front of him." 2

The pleasure-bound child becomes the reckless adult, a creature of impulse and whim. It was such youth who became known as the "now" generation of the sixties. The evidence suggests that many of these persons, though now well into their forties, continue to play a terrible price for their failed adaptive growth. And take the rest of us along with them.

The question becomes, how can parents best train the child to cope with life's normal unpleasures? How can the parent lead the child to master his anger, to tolerate tedium, to accept disappointment , to be brave about his uncertainties?

Developing Patience and Persistence in the Child

The first thing in grasping this nettle is to recognize that training the child is as important a part of being his parent as loving him.

Not all parents understand this. I see many parents who seem to feel that if they simply love their child and, in their own behavior, demonstrate self-control, concern for others, and acceptance of rational authority, these capacities will carry over into the child.

2   McArthur,Micky I'd Rather be Wanted than Had. Stoddart Publishing , Toronto, 1990.

This is not so. To be sure, some children are a whole lot harder to train to patience, persistence and self-control than others. This is a matter of temperament. Some children are intense and energetic. Such children require very determined parenting to lead them to patience and self-control. Other more placid child children respond well to average parental determination.

Two aspects of temperament seem particularly relevant determinants of how easy or difficult it will be to parent this particular child. These are activity level and intensity.

Activity Level: Some infants are so squirmy they need two hands and a foot on their chest to change their diapers, and bathing them is a liquid adventure for both participants. Other less energetic children don't disturb their bed covers when they sleep, lie quietly in their bath, and move slowly about the house. Obviously, these less active children will require a lot less parental input to train them than the overly active child.

Intensity: Some infants react intensely to life; whether that reaction be a negative or a positive one, it is intense. When such a child is hungry he screams and becomes so distressed that he cannot be distracted by holding or playing with him. Other infants are much more placid. If they are hungry they whimper, and they don't spit out food they don't like; they just hold it in their mouths and won't swallow.

Obviously the child who experiences every frustration intensely is going to have a harder time learning to tolerate unpleasure than the child for whom such events, while unpleasant perhaps, do not overwhelm.

So the energetic and intense child needs much more determined parenting input than the low-energy, placid child needs, and when children do not acquire tolerance for unpleasure at a normal rate, it is reasonable to ask just what kind of child was this mother given to rear.

Regardless of his temperament, the child must acquire a reasonable degree of tolerance for unpleasure if he is to cope with life. If he's energetic and intense then his mother is simply going to have to try harder.

The process of such training begins with the infant in his crib. He wakes hungry, and he cries. His mother puts the bottle on to heat. He must wait while the bottle heats. He must, for a few minutes, tolerate hunger and waiting. When he does, he practices waiting. And, eventually, the bottle arrives. His unpleasure goes away. And the process is repeated regularly.

What happens to the child immersed in this process? He practices waiting, and with practice waiting gets easier. As well, he learns that the bottle eventually arrives. At first he thought, 'This feeling is awful and, who knows, it may never go away.' But he finds it does. Regularly! Another thought then arises, 'The bottle arrived before; it will probably arrive again.' He becomes optimistic, which makes it is easier to wait.

This coping with moderate unpleasure continues and increases. Once the child gets on his feet, his mother must deny him sometimes. She says, "No, I can't play with you now, I have things on the stove." He either waits, or has a tantrum and ends contained. The enxt time he waits.

When the next child is born, more of Mother's time is taken up and even more limits have to be set. Each limit set, each expec-tancy communicated, requires the child to cope with unpleasure and stretches his tolerance a degree.

If Mother continues to serve the child excessively, saying perhaps, "OK, I'll pick up your toys, but just this once," not only does she fail to stretch the child's tolerance for unpleasure, but also she teaches him that Mother can be had. So it is that mothers,passing from the nurturance to the training phase of parenting, must harden their hearts. They must stop doing everything for the child.

This withdrawal of instant service on her part may well set omnipotence-devaluation in process. The child is a whole creature, and, at the same time as he is working out his omnipotence devalu-ation, he is coping with unpleasure. It is the mastery of such unpleas-ure generates patience and persistence, courage and self-control.

Let me close this chapter with a program designed to deal with a problem in which intolerance for unpleasure is a major component.

Getting Dressed in the Morning

Let's go back now to the anecdote with which we opened this chapter, the trouble Bryan's mother was having getting him dressed in the morning. In the context of how she might manage this more successfully, perhaps we can demonstrate how effective discipline develops tolerance for one of life's unpleasures, the unpleasure of tedious expectation. As we shall see this also serves to disillusion infantile omnipotence and diminish egocenticity .

Remember Mother had dispatched Bryan to school, a cold piece of toast in his hand and tears in his eyes? And we knew that next morning it was just going to be more of the same.

What is Mother doing wrong? Is there some way she can manage the situation more effectively? Let's deal with the first question first.

Mother has slipped into a very common mode of poor discipline which I call ineffective over control. It is ineffective because it doesn't work. Oh, it does get Bryan dressed in the morning, but tomorrow when the sock sticks it will be more of the same. And tomorrow. And tomorrow. And tomorrow. It is over control because Mother is always there standing over the child, supervising , cajoling, assisting, nagging, and eventually, thundering and lightning at him.

Bryan hates ineffective over control, and so does his mother, but she feels she has no choice. "If I didn't stand over him, he'd be late for school every morning, and he'd never get any breakfast. The social worker will be after me for sending him to school hungry."

Mother, doing what she feels she must, has slipped into a vicious cycle. In the morning nagging and tears, followed by a miserable day for Mother ruminating over her morning anger such that she ends telling herself, "Tomorrow morning, no matter what happens, I am not going to raise my voice to that child." No! Tomorrow she is going to be kind and firm and not get angry, no matter what.

The next morning comes and when the sock sticks, guess who ends up flat on his back, elaborating fantasies about that stain on the ceiling? Mother grits her teeth and controls her anger. She ends up dressing him but the worst that escapes her lips is a mildly intoned: "Do you think ... dear ... that tomorrow morning ... you might try ... just the tiniest bit harder to dress yourself without Mother standing over you?"

"Sure thing, Mom," Bryan replies, but Wednesday morning it's more of the same. This time Mother barely manages to keep her cool. It costs but, God bless her, she really tries.

Thursday morning she labors but she simply cannot stand it any longer. She erupts. The whole *schmear*, thunder, lightning, name calling, threats. In fact, as he is going out the door she is telling him of her plan to take the afternoon plane to Peru and don't expect to find her there when he comes home.

By the time Bryan gets to school he has forgotten her threat, he's heard that kind of thing before. But at home the guilt is incredible. She spends the day marching about the house flagellating herself with a wet dish towel. By nightfall she is a terminally reformed epitome of dedicated motherhood. However, next morning the vicious cycle starts all over again.

What is Bryan learning from all this? You can be sure he is learning something, even if it isn't what Mother intended to teach him. Well, I've interviewed a lot of Bryans in my playroom and they usually perceive this situation thus.

"Why did your mother get so mad at you Thursday morning?" I ask.

"Thursday morning?" Bryan looks puzzled a moment and it is clear he doesn't immediately remember. Clearly he found the whole thing a lot less troubling than his mother did. "Oh yeah, she threw a real spazz."

"What made her so mad?" I ask again.

"Aw, she was just in a bad mood. She gets that way." He rolls his eyeballs and shrugs his shoulders.

"She told me the reason she got mad was because you didn't get dressed on time," I say.

"Nope," Bryan shakes his head. "Couldn't be that. She didn't get mad at me Monday. I didn't get dressed on time Tuesday and she didn't get mad. I didn't get dressed on time Wednesday and she didn't get mad. All she did was ask me to hurry up a whole lot of times. Naw! She was just in a bad mood." He gives me a knowing look, "You know how women are."

Bryan has learned something about this woman. He has learned that if you don't get dressed on time in the morning, three times out of four the worst that will happen is that Mother will get a little antsy. With those kinds of odds going for you, why worry? He has learned you don't have to do what Mother says until the thunder and lightning starts.

Mother doesn't want to have to lose her temper just to get Bryan to move. Even so, that is what she has taught him.

More important still is what Bryan has not learned. He has not learned how to persist when the going gets a little tough. He has not learned to accommodate to others, not learned that his mother is a person with rights, towards whom he ought to be occasionally con-siderate. He has not accepted her rational authority and learned that to obey is not necessarily disgraceful or demeaning. In short, his adaptive growth has lagged.

What ought to be happening? What if when Mother called Bryan in the morning he leaped from bed, brushed his teeth, combed his hair and got dressed by eight o'clock without being reminded, threatened, or punished. How much better for Mother's nerves this would be!

When things go well with discipline, this is where one expects to be with a nine year old. But getting there is a staged process. One expects to take the five year old through the dressing process step by step. "Put on your shorts, now your shirt. Here, I'll help you with the buttons. What a big boy you're getting, able to dress yourself." Later, it's laying out the clothes and leaving the child to do the main parts himself, and still later it becomes "be done by eight o'clock and don't forget to brush your teeth."

As the child grows older and more able, Mother moves her supervision back a notch, leaving more to the child. Eventually a little praise and encouragement when he succeeds and a little disapproval when he dawdles is enough to keep things in motion.

But things do not always proceed this easily; some children need more vigorous training than that. Furthermore, some mothers are not consistent, and, running late, will dress the child when he is well able to do the job himself. Some mothers are not clear enough about their expectations, or not determined enough to persist in the face of his reluctance. "Perhaps he's not ready to do it himself," they wonder, and they end dressing him.

For a variety of reasons, mothers can slip into standing over a nine year old and saying, "Put on your shirt. Put on your shorts. Pull on your socks." Step by step they supervise him. This is treating a nine year old as though he were four or five. This may get him dressed, but it will not lead him to do the job himself, nor will it promote his adaptive growth. Still mothers feel they have no choice. "If I did not stand over him, he'd be late for school every day."

If Mother and Bryan were my regular patients, and I had decided this was a good place to begin a little remedial parenting, I would begin by asking Mother, "Can Bryan dress himself?"

"Of course he can," she would undoubtedly reply. "If he's in a hurry to go to his friend's house, he can dress in a flash."

"Then expecting him to dress in the morning isn't an unreasonable expectation?"

"Of course not. Other children do it all the time without their mothers standing over them."

"Then let's insist upon it. Let's say to Bryan, 'it's your job to get dressed in the morning . . . without supervision . . . and I expect you to do it from now on. Furthermore, getting dressed means: underwear; two socks, matching, one on each foot; shirt buttoned; shoes on and tied; and don't forget your belt.' "

Mother smiles. She recognizes that there is a tendency among nine year olds to regard socks and belts as optional attire.

"You have to spell it out," I tell her, "or sure as shooting he's gonna say, 'You didn't say I had to wear socks,' or possibly, 'Shoes tied wasn't part of the deal.'"

At this point most mothers bring up other morning duties such as washing his face, brushing his teeth, combing his hair, making his bed, putting his dirty clothes in the hamper and pajamas away. After some discussion we agree that for now we will only program one thing, getting dressed, agreeing that if we try to correct all of his shortcomings at once, we would overwhelm him and probably fail. We can come back to those other things later.

"Now we have made it clear what he is to do, we need to set a time limit on it being done."

"Time limit?" Mother queries.

"Yes, a time limit. Unless you'd prefer to continue nagging?"

Mother shakes her head vigorously.

After some discussion we decide the job should be finished by eight o'clock which gives him plenty of time to dress, get his breakfast, and be out the door so as not to be late for school. It also allows a little extra time to supervise if we have to.

Now we have to make sure he has a way of knowing how much time he has left. With a nine year old that's easy, you just put a clock in his room. With other children you may have to use a radio, saying "When the news comes on you've three minutes left." With even younger children you put a timer in the room. "When the buzzer goes off you've got three more minutes to be dressed."

What you must not do is remind him of the time yourself. "Bryan, it's seven minutes to eight. Bryan it's five minutes to eight. Bryan it's four minutes to eight." That's nagging, and it's what you are trying to get out of doing.

Now he knows precisely what he is to do and when it is to be done by.

What Mother must do now is leave him to do it. Mother is not to call, remind, come up, ask, peek, or send up his little brother to see how things are going. She is to leave him alone to do the job because our goal is to have him dress himself without supervision.

"He won't dress, you know," Mother says.

"I think you are right," I reply. I use the word *think* because some children, when warned about the planned program, do an overnight turnabout, but most don't, and she is probably right, he won't dress.

"So what am I supposed to do, let him be late for school?" Mother asks.

"No sir! It's his duty to go to school and yours to make sure he gets there. So, at eight o'clock you go up and supervise. You'll probably find him flat on his back, one sock stuck at the heel, lost in space. Don't yell. Don't scold. Take a seat. Get comfortable and supervise. 'Put on your shorts, put on your pants.' Item by item, step by step you supervise him, just as though he were five years old."

"How will that grow him up?"

"Supervision doesn't, but you have no choice, so you are doing what you are forced to do as quickly and conveniently as possible . So long as you stay in the room there with him he'll keep going and in another six or seven minutes he'll be dressed."

"Then what?" Mother asks.

"Then you say to him, 'Bryan, it isn't my job to stand over you and get you dressed, not at your age. Furthermore, I have a lot of other things to do. Even so, I've had to come up here and supervise you, which is not fair to me. So, every morning at eight o'clock when I come up, if you are not dressed, I'll supervise you, but that will cost you.'"

"'You mean you are going to charge me for supervision?' Bryan will reply, astounded at the idea."

"Explain to him, 'Bryan, by charge, I mean there will be a consequence. You will lose half an hour of a selected privilege, and I select the privilege. And that is the way it is going to be every morning until you've learned to get dressed on time.'"

"'What privilege are you gonna select?' Bryan will ask, a calculating look in his eye. You don't have to answer him, and often it's best not to, at least not right then. Tell him 'I'll let you know later.'"

The punishment, or consequence for those who feel more comfortable with a euphemism, is given because he required supervision to complete his task. For the sake of illustration, let's suppose we decided to penalize him half an hour TV time after supper on days he doesn't get dressed on time without supervision.

This is what I call the reinforcer. It is action communication which, speaking louder than words, underlines the parent's determination.

Now that I have given you all the elements let me summarize the program in a table.

GETTING DRESSED IN THE MORNING
Clear expectation
Set a time limit
Supervise if necessary
Consequence for supervision
Persist to train

Probable Course of Events

I tell mothers the probable course of events. I do this because it almost always happens exactly this way, which reassures the mother and makes her more responsive to my future directions. This is what I tell her.

"The first morning when you arrive at eight o'clock he will be lying flat on his back on the bed, one sock half over his heel. You will have to supervise him step by step but you will keep your cool. It's a lot more nervous-making to stand in the kitchen wondering if he is getting dressed and going up every ten minutes to see than it is to tell yourself, Well, whether he is or not I've got a plan. At eight o'clock I'm going to take care of it. Till then I'm not gonna fret.' And when eight o'clock comes you've organized the ten minutes so you aren't frantic about the baby or the burnt toast."

"Now you supervise him, and you'll manage not to yell. He will be dressed by eight-ten, which leaves ample time to get him off to school. He may not have dressed himself, but he does get out the door without shouts and tears, which is a big step to cooling some of the tensions."

"That night, when it comes time to lose his half hour TV, he will look at you nonchalantly and say, with studied poise, 'As a matter of fact, I didn't intend to watch TV tonight. I had other plans.' And he'll go in his room and read, or play with the dog, or find something else reasonably interesting to do."

This tends to infuriate and dismay parents and indeed leads many of them to utter that famous lament of terminally frustrated grown-ups. "It's no use punishing, because nothing bothers him."

I warn them about this **sweet lemon** technique and tell them neither to escalate the punishment nor to give up on it.

"Stick to the plan," I tell mothers. "In time he'll change his tune."

The second morning when Mother arrives in his room at eight o'clock, he will again be flat on his back, checking out the stain on the roof, the sock barely over his toes. But again, Mother is to keep her cool and supervise him, and he will make it out the door without tears. That night when punished he will say, "As a matter of fact, I wasn't planning to watch TV tonight." Then he will find a comic book, bring it out to the kitchen and, while Mother is washing dishes, walk up and down turning pages and laughing uproariously at the comic strips.

The third morning when Mother arrives the sock may be on, but he won't be finished. Some other stumbling block will have felled him. Probably he will utter some eloquent excuse, "I couldn't find another shirt; and the one you laid out I can't wear because every time I do I get bad marks in spelling."

Mothers should ignore such gambits, stay cool and supervise, perhaps wish him better luck tomorrow morning.

"That's not fair," he will protest. "I was half dressed. I should only get half a punishment."

Mother should tell him it was a nice try, but no way. He has but one simple duty to accomplish and lots of time. Since he didn't make it, he gets the whole punishment and that's that. He may complain a little but chances are that, for a change, breakfast will be a relatively amicable occasion.

That night, when it comes time to punish him, Mother won't hear the "I wasn't going to watch TV" spiel. This time he will get mad. "You've no right to take away my TV. That's my favorite show. Every kid on the street is watching that show. As a matter of fact, my teacher assigned it for homework."

If he can't bully his mother out of the punishment he may try another tack. "Tell you what, Mom, you let me watch that program tonight and I absolutely guarantee you I will get dressed on time tomorrow."

Mothers who buy this con end with egg on their faces. The right answer is this: "Tell you what, son. You be dressed tomorrow morning before the buzzer sounds, and you'll be watching TV this time tomorrow night."

The fourth morning when Mother goes up he will be dressed. She won't have to supervise him and that night she won't have to punish him.

The fifth morning, as Mother mounts the stairs, he will call, "Walk slow, I'm almost finished." The next morning, the sixth, when Mother arrives in his room she will find him flat on his back on the bed, sock stuck at the heel, lost in space again.

Why did we lose it? Because he hasn't been punished for two days. The consequence, not having been recently suffered, has lost its urgency. So he lapses.

At this point Mother must do exactly what the program calls for. That is, she must supervise without scolding and offer the usual punishment that evening. She must not give him another chance, must not say to him, "I am not going to punish you tonight because you did so well for a couple of days, but I am counting on you getting dressed properly tomorrow morning. You will, won't you dear?"

It is essential that the same behavior always results in the same consequence if the training message is to embed itself in his developing persona.

It usually takes three weeks before the program is working most of the time. Mind you, if the program started on a Monday, the sixth day will be a Saturday morning. He doesn't have to go to school Saturday and Sunday, so shouldn't we forget the program until Monday? No way! Two days is too long a gap in an initial training program. It's OK to change the ready time to nine o' clock because it's the weekend, but the program should otherwise remain the same.

By the fifth week the child is making it five days out of six without supervision or punishment, which is normal for nine year olds.

Remember, getting dressed in the morning was not the primary agenda; it was the vehicle to lead us to our real goal. Our goal was to grow him up, to promote his adaptive growth in the area of coping with tedium.

When we began, pulling his sock over his heel was more unpleasure than Bryan could master, but now he is doing it most of the time. We have stretched his tolerance for tedium just a trifle.

Other things have happened to. When Mother charged him for having to supervise him she sent him an action message. That message said, "I am a person with rights. You must come to recognize that and accommodate to me sometimes." He did so accommodate and in doing so became a little less egocentric than he had been.

Furthermore, by setting a clear limit and finding a way to make him meet it, or be punished, Mother exercised her reasonable parental authority. She was not overbearing. Neither was she capricious, weak or inconsistent. It is such steady authority which disillusions a child's omnipotence.

Capricious or overbearing authority is hard to accept; it has too much of the "I'll show you who's boss" tone, and children are bound to resist it. Weak or inconsistent authority does not have to be accepted; it can be evaded.

In this instance, Mother has been planfully firm. She has succeeded in demonstrating the difference between an adult's and a child's prerogatives. Giving her child an experience of rational authority, she has led him a step down the road to giving up his omnipotent illusion and accepting his childhood.

And when, after a couple of months getting dressed in the morning is not a problem, the program will no longer be necessary. Then, one morning her child will say, with pride in his voice, "Hey, Mom, you notice how I always get dressed on time in the mornings now?" This, as we shall now learn, is a brick of self-esteem settling in place.

Which brings us to the subject of our next chapter: the fourth cardinal characteristic of the omnipotent child, his sadly deficient self-esteem.

5

The Wounding of Pride

Seven-year-old Peter was giving me an account of all the adult things he deemed himself capable of doing.

"I could beat my father at bowling if I really tried," he declared. "I could shoot a real gun. I could drive a car if I had to. I know how to steer. I know where the brakes are . . . and the gas."

He paused, anticipating contradiction I suppose. Receiving none and having exhausted all examples of estimable power that came to mind, he summed up his position in this pithy way, "I can do anything adults can do, except adultery."

Keeping a straight face is an essential ingredient of the practice of child psychiatry and we child psychiatrists get lots of practice. So, with a grave countenance, I asked him, "What's adultery?"

"You know," he replied, giving me one of those how-dumb-can-you-get looks, "filling out income tax forms and all that junk."

Like most omnipotent children, Peter is minimally aware of the considerable discrepancy between his adult aspirations and his child capacities. But this statement says more about Peter than simply that an omnipotence illusion is alive and well in his psyche. It says something about his self-esteem.

Why is Peter volunteering this grandiose self-appraisal? He is boasting, trying to impress me with his competence, trying to induce me to appreciate and admire his illusory power. However, as such statements usually do, his has an opposite effect; it reveals his uncertainty about himself, tells the perceptive another thing,that his self-esteem is fragile.

Problems with self-esteem are characteristic of children caught up in that pattern of adaptive growth failure I call the Omnipotent Child Syndrome. Unlike the other three cardinal characteristics, self-esteem is not an adaptive competence. It is not a capacity to cope. Self-esteem is a by-product of adaptive growth. When adaptive growth does not proceed well we get adaptive weakness and poor self-esteem.

Manifestations of Poor Self-Esteem

Sometimes the child expresses his dismay about himself directly. He comes slumping in from school one day when the children have been particularly cruel or rejecting. Instead of uttering his usual torrent of vengeful fantasy, he is a picture of woebegone misery, declaring, "I'm dumb. I can't do anything right. Nobody likes me. I'm the weakest kid in the class."

It is on such an occasion that Mother first learns her son has a nickname such as Screwy or Stinky or Pampers, or some derogatory perversion of his surname.

Parents are more distressed about the damaged self-esteem of the omnipotent child than all of his other characteristics. I regularly hear them say things like, "I'd do anything if I could just help him to like himself."

They try to find some area of success for him. "If he could just be really good at one thing I'm sure it would do wonders for him."

They agonize about how he got this way. "It isn't as though we don't try to find things to praise him for; we try not to make comparisons or run him down."

They feel guilty. For years the child-rearing books have claimed, 'All that is necessary to lead a child to value himself is that his parents value him.' So, recollecting moments of anger, they wonder if they have valued him enough.

It is simply not true that parental approval is the principal generator of self-esteem in the child. We shall deal with this in detail later. For the moment, let me get back to some other ways in which damaged self-esteem is manifest in the Omnipotent Child.

Many children cover their damaged self-esteem by extravagant declarations of worth, such as that made by Peter. To those who do not know the child well, he may seem more in danger of developing a superiority rather than an inferiority complex.

As Peter illustrated, these children entertain profoundly unrealistic self-expectations. They aspire to all the competencies of adulthood. Because they have not sacrificed their omnipotent illusion they feel they must be the equal of adults. "I could beat you at chess," they declare, and then prove to have no idea how the pieces move.

So long as their omnipotent illusion demands that they compete on an equal basis with adults, they are bound to lose, are they not?

Another way in which these children's exquisite sensitivity about their worth reveals itself is in their inability to accept second place whether that means losing a game, taking their place in line, or perhaps even getting the shorter of two pencils or the smaller sheet of drawing paper.

Playing games with children soon reveals their uncertain self-esteem. Omnipotent children cannot lose, and if this seems imminent they change the rules, cheat, or accuse others of cheating. Once losing seems inevitable, they either quit playing or start playing foolishly. One child with whom I used to play checkers would, when he realized he was about to lose, manage to knock over the board, thus preserving himself from the agony of defeat.

Because these children have not grown beyond magic forms of thinking, they come up with some quite ingenious modes of denying defeat. Faced with losing at checkers, one such child would refuse to take his second to last move, the one which would allow me to jump his last piece. It is as though by ending the game short of this point he prevented the loss.

Another gimmick this child turned to was to take his second to last move, and then take my move for me such that he ended up taking the last jump. Through a psychological alchemy available only to omnipotent children, he converted himself into the winner by taking his opponent's jump.

All of this behavior is designed to protect a self-esteem so fragile that even the most minor manifestations of second best cannot be tolerated.

As children grow older it becomes increasingly difficult for them to preserve their self-esteem in this fashion. A child must lose sometimes. When he does , he must acknowledge his limitations and find some way to accept them, or develop even more extensive and unrealistic methods of avoiding that reality.

One not uncommon method children select is to withdraw from competition. He rationalizes that withdrawal in a variety of ways. He may say, for example, "I could get the top mark in reading if I wanted to, but I don't care about that subject." Similarly, if he tries base ball and can't immediately be one of the best, he decides that baseball is dumb and drops out.

Many such children stop playing with peers and begin to play with younger children where their skills are superior and they win easily. Ot they may choose to socialize with adults, who will make allowances for them. (Maybe even throw them a game?) Either way, they avoid peer comparisons.

There are a number of other psychological maneuvers these children use in order to protect their fragile self-esteem. There is the Walter Mitty Solution: withdrawal into fantasies of heroic achievement. There is the Sour Grapes Solution: denying the worth of an accomplishment one fears is beyond his grasp. Finally there is the Expert Solution: narrowing the scope of one's effort to some limited area of competence and then regarding that pursuit as the only significant measure of worth.

An adult example of the latter might be the tennis pro who whittles the senator down to size by declaring, "But he has a lousy backhand."

What has happened to such children is that they have not coped, so have not managed to construct an adequate sense of their own worth. They have a fragile self-esteem, and devote much of their life energy to concealing from themselves, and the world, their psychologically crippled state. In time many of them give up, withdraw from competition and settle for truncated lives.

They are the wounded in pride and their numbers are legion.

The Genesis of Self-Esteem

We need to ask what psychological events in infancy and early childhood lead a child to a comfortable sense of his own worth and give him self confidence. Before laying this out, we need to define a term and clarify a common misunderstanding.

Let's begin with the definition of the word "pride." Funk & Wagnall's dictionary list six definitions, of which two concern us. These are:

[1] An undue sense of one's own superiority;

[2] A proper sense of personal dignity and worth.

The first is false pride. It has been condemned by the Bible and seen in literature as the tragic flaw which brings down the hero.

What we are talking of here is not pride, it is vanity. It involves measures designed to impress, to force the world to validate one's pretensions of worth. The worth involved comes from **without**, not **within.**

The second definition, "a proper sense of personal dignity and worth," is true pride, a sense of personal worth that comes from within.

Let's us be clear on this, no one wants to turn out haughty and arrogant children; indeed we wish the very opposite. What we wish for our children is that second form of pride, that quiet self-assurance that comes from an inner sense of worth.

The serious misunderstanding is that parents can **give** pride to children. Pride is not a gift. It is a thing one earns through coping. The only way a parent can give a child self esteem is to lead him to cope . . . not do things for him, but make sure one's expectation is within his powers and then hold firm until he meets it.

I am forever confronted with guilt-laden mothers and fathers sure that somehow their child's failure to value himself arises from a lack of love or concern on their part. Please, understand, I am talking about loving parents. The other kind don't come to me. I am talking of persons who care very much about their child, too much perhaps. They have focussed so strongly on the child's feelings, in a desire to protect him from unpleasures, that they have failed him in another area, the area of discipline and training.

They feel the problem has to do with loving the child. However, the very act of seeking out a child psychiatrist's help is a statement of valuing the child.

What has confused these parents is that they know there are moments when they do not feel very loving towards the child, moments which stand out as beacons of guilt overshadowing that daily concern and commitment to the child that tells the real story.

My definition of parental love has to do with that commitment to the child, that action dialogue that says, "I am your person in the world. I am here for you, and no matter how tough the sledding gets, and I will be here for you so long as you need me." It isn't liking the child that counts. It's being committed to him.

There are the other kind of parents, the kind who love with the lips and not the heart. When the going gets tough, they get going—in some other direction. Of course their unloved child, has little chance of developing adequate self-esteem, but then he has little chance of developing many other psychological strengths as well.

The point is that love is not enough to generate healthy self-esteem in a child. Love is an essential ingredient, but it is insufficient of itself to produce a child with a proper sense of his own dignity and worth. How then is self-esteem truly generated?

Self-esteem is constructed during early childhood. It is built by the child himself. The building blocks are experiences of **mastery**, each of which stems from an instance of coping with normal growing-up expectations.

All children, when faced with the expectation that they learn to tie their shoes, say, "I can't, you do it for me." And they can't. Their fingers cannot manipulate the shoelaces successfully. However, skills develop very quickly in little children, and it takes much less practice for them to acquire a skill than it does us slower adults.

So Mother says, "Sure you can. Come on. I'll show you." She takes the ends of the laces, pulls them taut across one another. "See, you make an X. See the X?" At this point the child usually becomes interested in seeing the X, so Mother goes on, "Now you tuck one end through the bottom of the X." She helps the child to do that.

Perhaps the first day she doesn't get much past this point, but that's all right. Learning is one step at a time process.

The next day when Mother says, "Come on, let's tie your shoes," the child says, "I can't, you do it for me." But Mother persists and they have another five-minute shoe-tying session, with him making the X and Mother going on to explain how to make the loop.

So it goes, each morning the child protests a little, but Mother leads him through the task, helping, completing, watching, as gradually his fingers handle the laces more adeptly. Eventually, perhaps after six or seven such mornings, the child ties his shoes the whole way himself.

Then he will smile with pleasure and jump up and down proclaiming, "I can tie my shoes." Of course his loosely tied shoes may come undone in the process of jumping up and down, but this will have little effect upon his joy. "I can tie my shoes," he will declare to anyone who will listen, and when his father comes home that is the first thing he will hear.

What has happened? The child has encountered an expectation. Because he had never done that particular thing before, he drew back from the challenge, but Mother led him through the task, turning it over to him by degrees. Eventually he did it all by himself. He coped. He experienced mastery. He laid down a brick of self esteem.

Mastery means being able to do something real. It may not be a great something but it is real and he has done it. There is a feeling that accompanies experiences of mastery. Like all feelings it is basically indescribable.

However the feeling is pleasant. It has a component involve a sensation of strength or capability. It has been called, 'Joy in being a cause.' This feeling is the emotional core of self-esteem.

Mastery stands in opposition to the omnipotence illusion, for it involves real, not illusory, power. It is much more satisfying. The child has managed something real, and he knows he has. There are but a few things small children can do. When they manage one, the victory is sweet.

There are many tasks of development which offer the growing child opportunities for mastery. Some are mechanical such as learning to tie his shoes, to feed himself, to cut with scissors. Others are fragments of psychological adaptation: controlling his temper, holding back tears, waiting for his turn, understanding another person's point of view.

Each expectation coped with stretches the child's competence and builds his esteem. After three or four successful copings the child is much less liable to say, "I can't, you do it for me." Inside himself he is remembering, "I coped with the last four things that came my way; I can probably cope with this one too." So it is that self-confidence builds with each experience of mastery. It is in this sense that self-esteem is constructed by the child out of the building blocks of repeated experiences of mastery.

What of the child who has seemed so overwhelmed and woebegone that his sympathetic mother has tied his shoes for him or picked up most of his toys because he said, "I'm tired. You do it for me."?

He doesn't cope. He experiences no mastery. He builds no self-esteem.

Furthermore, after four expectations evaded, the child's inner statement becomes, "I couldn't cope with the last four things that came my way, and I probably can't cope with this one either." Instead of coming to feel self-confidence; he has come to feel self-doubt.

Expecting to fail, such children don't try hard, which of course leads to the failure anticipated and to more self-doubt. In time the child becomes an avoider. He doesn't want to try new things, and he covers up his apprehension by bad-mouthing the skill: "Aw, hockey's dumb. Who wants to play that stupid game?" So it is that non-coping not only fails to build esteem and confidence but also actively builds a poor image of self and undermines self-confidence.

For the child who is desperately trying to preserve his illusion of omnipotence, the situation is further aggravated. Trying to be the equal of adults, the child is setting up impossible standards and aspirations for himself. He cannot win at skill games because he is but a child with limited understanding and experience. He cannot equal the physical performance of the stronger adult. In all respects he is inferior to the adult: weaker, less experienced, untrained, with as yet undeveloped mental capacities. If he challenges the adult's competence, he is bound to lose.

However, the child who has accepted his childhood is not upset by his parents' superior competence. "When I'm as big as you," he says to his father, "I'll be able to bowl strikes too, won't I, Dad?"

Not so the omnipotent child. He fights fiercely not to acknowledge any form of adult superiority. "Kids are as good as grown-ups," Dewey insists. "Why should I have to go to bed at nine o'clock? You stay up late. Why can't I smoke a cigarette? You do! Why should I have to take math? I'm gonna be a hockey player when I grow up.

So long as Dewey clings to the omnipotence illusion he will see childhood as a devalued state. He cannot know that once he accepts his childhood, he will no longer need to judge himself against adult power. Paradoxical as it may sound, the route to true pride runs through the foothills of humility.

The Generation of Self-Esteem

All four of the adaptive competencies develop in concert with one another. When one fails to develop, the others are impaired also. This is particularly so with respect to self-esteem which, as we have seen, is not an adaptive competence but a by-product of successful adaptive maturation. Let me remind you of this by recalling a few of our earlier examples.

When Mother set up a program to deal with Terry's temper tantrums, her primary purpose was to wean the child away from his omnipotent illusion. When he began to control his temper prior to being removed to his room, he was not only accepting his mother's authority, but also he was stretching his self-control and diminishing his egocentricity. Furthermore, when Terry finally stopped having tantrums, one day he said to his mother, "Mom, have you noticed I don't fuss anymore?" He had experienced mastery and he had laid down a brick of self-esteem.

Similarly when Johnny's Second Telling Program had begun to work, he was coping with the unpleasure of coming when called, he was accommodating to his mother, and he was accepting her authority. Chances are one day he too said to her, "Hey, Mom, you notice I only got two second telling chips all week?" He too has known mastery and built a little self-esteem.

When Bryan's mother set up a program to get him to dress in the morning, her intention was to stretch his tolerance for tedium. However, when he succeeded in getting ready on time regularly, he announced to her, "I always get dressed in time in the morning now, don't I, Mom?" This too is real pride, is it not?

So it is that programs designed to promote adaptive growth in the child effect all three adaptive competencies, and generate self-esteem.

> Discipline leads to coping.
> Coping leads to mastery...
> Mastery builds self esteem.

Before we go on, let me say one more thing. Many adults do not enjoy good self esteem. For some of these this is a residue from childhood. But self esteem is an ongoing thing. You can't just sit on your laurels. You have to cope with today's challenges too.

People who give up easily, who are in the habit of copping-out when things get difficult, continually re-inforce their sense of their own worthlessness. I see quite a few mother's like this. I don't let them cop-out, if I can help it.

When a mother comes to me she often feels ashamed of her failure as a parent. But she did summon up enough courage to put her pride on the line and come. so we have a start.

When mother and I work out some management programs and I meet her weekly for a few visits to keep things rolling, the programs usually begin to work. Dewey stops having tantrums. He gets dressed in the morning.

He is coping with growing up. She is coping with motherhood. Not everywhere but enough to give her hope that someday things will be right on track.

It was tough but she did it. She coped, she mastered and she feels good about herself, maybe for the first time in years. In no time I hear she spreading her wings a little, taking another run at a couple of non- parenting things that defeated her last time out. Maybe I'm kidding myself, but I like to think that the child isn't the only one who benefits from our little adventure in remedial parenting.

Now that I have described the elements of the Omnipotent Child Syndrome it is time to put it all together and come to an understanding of exactly how the whole of adaptive growth proceeds and how it has gone wrong with Lydia, Frank and Dewey.

6

How Dewey Got That Way

The Nature of Diagnosis

In psychological medicine, a constellation of behavioral characteristics commonly occuring in company with one another is called
a syndrome. In the last four chapters I described the four cardinal
characteristics which make up the Omnipotent Child Syndrome.

THE CARDINAL CHARACTERISTICS
The Omnipotence Illusion
Retained Egocentricity
Intolerance for Unpleasure
Poor Self-Esteem

The earliest form of diagnosis is a symptom given a name. For
example School Phobia, Behaviour Disorder, Encopresis (Soiling) are
three such diagnoses.

Most children exhibiting such symptom diagnoses demonstrate
the cardinal characteristics of the Omnipotent Child Syndrome.
Furthermore one, another or all of these four incompetencies can be

seen to be causally related to the symptom in most instances. For example, the child who refuses to go to school, is trying to avoid an unpleasure which feels overwhelming to him. Often that unpleasure involves a challenge to his omnipotent illusion emanating from a teacher who is not prepared to let him make his own rules in the classroom. To want his way, rather than accommodate to the group, suggests a certain egocentricity of attitude, does it not?

Most psychological symptoms in children can be related to the underlying adaptive immaturity. Symptoms are minimally successful copings. Successful coping with normal growing up depends upon having acquired that degree of adaptive competence necessary to cope with the widening life expectancies the child encounters.

To summarize briefly; the Omnipotent Child Syndrome is a constellation of adaptive immaturity. Adaptively immature children lack the psychological equipment to cope with the normal expectations of home, the peer group and school. What they do is the best they can. The result is some patch-up solution to the growing up problem. Most psychological symptoms are patch-up solutions.

Diagnosis and Treatment

The purpose of diagnosis is to give direction to treatment. Diagnosis at the symptom level gives us little understanding to guide treatment. However, diagnosis based upon an adaptive competence model, such as underlies the omnipotent child syndrome, does lay out our options for us. It tells us we have two choices. We may either;

[1] Reduce the stress or
[2] Increase the child's adaptive competence.

If a child is living in a brutal and neglecting family, the stress is everything, and it must be addressed. If possible! Since this very often means making substitute rearing arrangements, and few facilities for such care exist, unreared children turning into violent or addictive adults are very much with us.

However, as I have illustrated repeatedly, the omnipotent children appearing in my practice come from reasonable families. Their stress is minimal. Their adaptive incompetence is profound.

The remedy for such children is adaptive retraining. The parents need to take the child through the adaptive growth cycle that failed first time around. They need professional guidance to do this. It is the child psychiatrist's job to provide that guidance.

Other Views

While this view seems correct and logical to me, many child psychiatrists do not see the problems in these terms.

There are still many child psychiatrists who feel the child's symptoms are due to psychological traumas repressed during early childhood. Treatment for them means involving the child in therapy intended to bring the repressed to the surface and strip it of its power.

There are others who see the family as sick, not the child and address their interventions to the family unit, not the individual. They deal with the fact that other children in the family are doing well, by calling this child the identified patient, which is a bit like calling him the family scapegoat.

More recently there are many who simply call all childen with behavioral symptoms Attention Deficit Disorder and give them Ritalin. (See Appendix A)

As you can see, I do not agree with any of these approaches. In my view, adaptive incompetence comes first and the symptom second. Let me spell that out in a little more detail.

How Dewey Really Got That Way.

The omnipotent child's problem is adaptive immaturity. It is **immaturity** because the child's ways would be acceptable were he four or five years old, but he is far too impatient, self-centered, and willful to cope with what the world reasonably expects of a nine-year-old. It is **adaptive** because the capacities we are concerned with are those crucial to coping with life in a society with expectations and rules.

The omnipotent child is trying to cope with a nine-year-old's world using the adaptive equipment of a pre-schooler.

"But, underneath it all, Dewey is an unhappy boy, is he not?" parents ask. Of course Dewey is unhappy. He's in the soup with his mother all the time, the teacher's on his case every day and no-one wants to play with him. However, Dewey's unhappiness is a **result** of his problem, not its **cause**. Treatment of his unhappiness is not treating cause, it is alleviating a symptom.

Let me illustrate with a clinical example. Dewey is often rejected or teased by his peers. He can't get along with them because he is too self-centered to accommodate to their playtime agenda, too impatient and insensitive to play properly. He offends without realizing. They tell him to buzz off. Of course, he is unhappy to be rejected like this.

If the child psychiatrist deals with this unhappiness by uncovering its source - peer rejection - and ventilating Dewey's distress, he will reduce the present tension. He has let the pus out of the boil and Dewey will feel better.

But this does not solve the basic problem. Until Dewey acquires the patience to take his turn and moves out of the egocentricity that renders him insensitive in social situations, he will simply offend all over again. In a couple of weeks peer failures will have generated the tension again. The pus is back in the boil.

Dewey needs adaptive growth more than he needs emotional relief.

The same kind of tension is continually rising at home. Even though Mother truly cares about Dewey, ninety percent of the exchanges between them are negative in tone. Dewey feels unloved, and Mother doesn't feel very loving. This is easy to detect, and therapists with shallow understanding leap on it as the cause of the problem. They tell Mother that what Dewey needs is more love.

For months Mother has been trying her hardest to love Dewey despite his difficult ways. To tell her to be more loving is not only to increase her guilt, but also it misleads her as to the cause of Dewey's problem. It certainly contains no usable parenting advice. How can she be more loving when she is trying her best and regularly coming up empty?

The simple fact is, if Dewey is ever going to get more love from Mother he is first going to have to become a lot more lovable. So long as he is as impatient and demanding, rude and arrogant, Mother will, her strongest resolve to the contrary, end angry with him on many, many occasions.

The short answer to all this is that it was not the loving that failed, it was the training that went wrong. It needs to be done again. This is what I call remedial parenting.

It has been my experience that you can tell people what they did wrong if, in the next breath you are prepared to tell them how to do it better. That is my office approach and that is my approach in this book. So, if you see yourself in some of the scenarios I describe, don't despair. I am going to walk the rest of that mile with you.

There are two important variables that determine how a given training encounters will work out, the effectiveness of the training measures utilized and the temperament of the child. Let's deal with the second first.

The Role of Temperament in Child Development

Let me re-iterate; Deweys are made, not born. It is true temperament plays a role in determining what kind of an individual the child will become, but in most cases temperament is not the principal determining factor. God deals each of us a hand of cards, but it is parenting which gives us the skill to play those cards well or poorly.

Temperamentally intense, energetic infants and toddlers are much more likely to hit the terrible twos with a bang. In my practice at least three out of four pre-school children brought to me because the terrible twos were continuing, have been lively and intense from birth.

Though it makes children harder to rear, a lively temperament can become an asset in adult life. The intense infant may become an adult who feels things more passionately, who tackles life more vigorously. Such persons may be destined to become movers and shakers. However, there are probably more of them in jail than the other kind.

Some children are mild and accommodative from infancy. When they are five, 'Aw, shucks' is their response to major disappointment, and 'phooey' their angriest epithet. Ah, but to be blessed with such a child, you say? Well, these docile creatures have their problems too. They may not have temper tantrums, but they can learn to withhold their stool if their *not-so terrible twos* don't get worked through. On the other hand, their style may lead them into contemplative ways, perhaps eventually to wisdom. The world needs its wise men as much as it needs movers and shakers. These days, perhaps more.

Parents too have their temperaments which may suit them to rear one child and not another. Furthermore, parents have their situation. No child, even one in the same family, experiences exactly the same rearing environment. Some children are born when the parents are poor and own no expensive breakables that need protection. Young parents want the baby to go to bed so they can make out in the living room. Older parents tend to feel less urgent about such matters.

Parents learn how to parent by practicing on their first child. This usually means a certain amount of overprotection and over control. With the second they relax a little. By the fourth child Mother may have relaxed to the point one hears her saying things like, "Oh, don't worry. He'll be using his knife and fork by the time he's twenty-one."

What it comes down to is this, each Dewey is where he is because there has been a discrepancy between the rearing he, with his particular temperament, needed, and that he received.

That he received is the part we can do something about, so let's get to it.

The Parenting

It is reasonable to impose your will upon the child.
In fact it is your duty to do so. A major part of your job is to turn a natural barbarian into a social creature.

Not everybody agrees with this. There are persons who will tell you every child is naturally sweet, kind, generous and accommodative. For such persons, if he isn't acting this way, then the parents are not meeting his emotional needs.

When problem behavior occurs, the measures such persons propose always start by urging the parent to appreciate how the child feels and tailor their approach to alleviating his distress. If he's fearful at night, lie down with him. If he kicks a hole in the door, provide him with a kicking board. Even though the behavior is socially unacceptable no hint of disapproval should be permitted to color the mother's response.

Here is a true example. A parent of an intense and lively four year old reported that the instructor of her parenting course had advised advised her thus. In a fit of anger her child had opened the fridge and thrown every item, except one, onto the kitchen floor. "Compliment him on that fact that he left one item in the fridge," the instructor said.

That's like thanking Hitler for invading only half of France, is it not?

This instructor believes that social growth is as inevitable as physical growth so training is unnecessary. All that is necessary is to keep the peace and wait -- in a loving environment, the child will somehow osmose adaptive growth. 'Of course, if the child isn't maturing, obviously the environment wasn't loving enough.'

What a Catch 22 for mothers that is!

I dwell on this approach simply to label it nonsense. The normal infant, though he be as appealing as a puppy, is totally self-centered. He thinks he is boss of the world, and when he wants something he wants it now. He isn't bad, he's just a baby. And he will stay a baby if we continue to indulge his omnipotent ways. The truly loving thing is to grow him up so that he has a chance for a happy adult life.

When one looks deeply into the family life and early development of children like Dewey, one rarely finds real evidence of significant emotional neglect or rejection. Though Mother may be trying her hardest to love her child it soon comes to be that the air in her house is not laden with affection. Living with a Dewey erodes good will at a rate equal to if not exceeding that at which the Colorado River carved out the Grand Canyon.

Later, when Dewey declares, as all children do from time to time, "You don't love me anymore," Mother suspects he's right.

So it is that when a mother comes to my office with her Dewey in resistant tow, she is usually consumed with guilt, absolutely sure the problem is she doesn't love her child enough. Furthermore, she is devastated by a deep sense of failure. Chances are she was the woman who, when pregnant, had fantasized her eventual entry into the Book of World Records as the greatest mother since Eve.[1]

She's been angry at Dewey. Lots of times. Why? Because he won't do what she expects of him, because he is often rude, because he makes her feel such a failure. She has learned to mistake that anger for not loving him.

The *sine qua non* of loving the child is not being sweet and speaking softly on all occasions, nor hugging him when you feel like wringing his neck. It's both of you knowing you are going to hang around and do what you can for him until he's full grown, no matter how tough it gets. It is the parent's **commitment** to the child that is the essence of loving him.

The parents who come to my office love their child. If they didn't, they wouldn't be there. So no matter what the magazines say, Dewey isn't in trouble because his mother doesn't love him. He's in

1   Actually Eve's track record left a little something to be desired. That Cain of hers sounds like he had a few adaptive growth problems.

trouble because she can't figure out how to grow him up. The part that's giving her trouble is the part called discipline.

Discipline

Discipline has had a bad press in the last couple of decades. For the love-is-all-it-takes crowd, discipline has become a dirty word. Many of these persons equate discipline with punishment. And confuse punishment with the adjective punitive. So we need to clarify what discipline and punishment really are. Let's begin with a some definitions.

Webster defines discipline as *training which molds, strengthens, or perfects,* which is where the subtitle for this book came from. This is what that term refers to when used in this book.

Punishment is one of several methods by which discipline is **reinforced,** that is rendered impressive enough to communicate its message to the child. Other reinforcers include approval, disapproval, and reward.

Punitive is an adjective. With respect to child rearing, it refers to **mean** forms of punishment. Punishment is an essential, ingredient of discipline. **Mean** punishment has no place in child rearing.

Discipline is as essential to parenting as is nurturance. Children need both if they are to mature. A parental attitude which includes both in a balanced way is essential. Diana Baumrind 2calls this authoritative love.

Authoritative love includes both nurturance and discipline and avoids that polarization that seems to say loving the child somehow stands in opposition to disciplining him, when in fact discipline is a major expression of parental love.

There are four possibilities here.

---

2   Diana Baumrind, Institute of Child Development, University of California.

[1] If you love your child but do not discipline him, he may come to be sunny and see the world as a friendly place, but he won't learn to cope with it or with himself. He will be a *sunny non-coper.*

[2] If you offer your child lots of control, but do so coldly without adequate nurturance, without a true concern for his emotional well-being, he may learn to cope with the world, but he is unlikely to enjoy it. He will become a *sullen coper.*

[3] If you offer your child firm and effective controls in a context of care and commitment, he will become *a sunny coper.*

[4] If you offer your child minimal love, and minimal training, he becomes what I call an *unreared child.*

This produces either an angry, vengeful creature with serious adaptive incompetence, or an insatiable seeker of instant gratification. Many such youth are surfacing these days. Violent amorality is the name of the former's game, drug addiction the latter.

Here it is, summarized in a table.

LOVE AND DISCIPLINE
Love minus discipline => sunny non-coper
Discipline minus love => sullen coper
Love plus discipline => sunny coper
No love, no discipline => unreared child

In the case of the omnipotent child, the lack has been one of discipline. How did this come about.? Most parents try to discipline. Why didn't it work? How does one discipline effectively? What are the essential ingredients? How can parents provide these?

This is what the rest of this book is all about. At this point, all I want to do is provide enough overview to lead us into the principles of discipline.

The Disciplinary Process

Discipline involves two principal parental activities: setting limits and communicating expectations. Setting limits means saying some *no you can'ts* and communicating expectations means saying some *now you must.*

Setting limits is first undertaken to protect the toddler from physical dangers. An example might be telling the child not to touch the stove, or climb on the stair rail. Once he is on his feet and into things, many such forbiddings necessarily arise, though not all for his protection. "No, you can't throw your glass on the floor. I know it makes a pretty sound when it breaks, but you can't go through life breaking things just to hear what they sound like."

Whether Mother's motive be to protect her child or protect her property, setting limits intrudes upon the child's omnipotence illusion. As the child grows older and acquires greater knowledge of reality, there is less need to protect him with limits. However, since his capacity for destruction increases also, setting limits continues to be very much the name of the game.

Discipline with toddlers is *action dialogue.*

Don't tell the small child not to touch the stereo four times and then, when he does, scold and remove him. That teaches him you don't mean **no** until you get mad. Tell him no once, and the moment he takes a step toward the stereo pick him up and put him in his playpen for two minutes. A few of those trips and he will learn he only gets one **no** and then its in the cage for two minutes. *It is the action which teaches him, not the words.*

Communicating expectations means saying now you must. An example might be telling the toddler, "It's time you started helping to dress yourself. Look! I'll lay the shirt out on the bed for you so the arms won't get mixed up. Now, you slip your hands into the sleeves and pull it on. Then I'll help you with the buttons."

Occasions for communicating expectations increase as the child grows older and more capable of doing things for himself. For the five year old the instruction is "Put on your shirt and pants." When he's seven, it becomes "Get dressed and don't forget to brush your teeth." As the child grows older and his capacities increase, one expects more of him and leaves more of the detail to his choice.

Here also *action dialogue* is the preferred mode of communication. But this is harder to set up, especially with older children.

Given such approaches the terrible two's come to an end. The child develops some patience and self control. His egocentricity slowly diminishes and he makes his peace with childhood. This didn't happen for Dewey.

Dewey's training failed to promote his adaptive growth. Either there were not enough *no you cants* or *now you musts*, or they were not communicated effectively. So, it is necessary to go through the training again.

Of course he isn't a baby now and the simple measures that work for toddlers will not work for him. So we have to design measures that will. This is not as complicated as it sounds. There are a few simple principles to guide one. In the next chapter I shall deal with these principles in detail.

7

The Principles of Discipline

There are five principles of discipline I find relevant to child rearing. Let me enumerate these.

PRINCIPLES OF DISCIPLINE
Set a clear expectation
Set a time limit
Supervise if necessary
Apply a reinforcer
Persist to train

If we are to retrain an omnipotent child we shall have to design workable disciplinary programs. We cannot do this unless we understand the principles of discipline, so let's look at each of these in turn.

Principle Number One: Set a Clear Expectation

Suppose you have decided that you, your nine year old, and his room would all benefit from regular cleaning Saturday mornings. You have decided that a little planful firmness is in order, not only because a tidy room would be a considerable asset but also because you have detected in him a certain reluctance to tackle the tedious.

Your first job is to decide exactly what is reasonable to expect of a nine year old and then consider how to communicate that expectation to the child.

If you were merely to say to him, "I want you to clean your room on Saturdays," you would **not** be setting a clear expectation.

It is likely something like this would happen. He would sweep the assorted items cluttering the floor under his bed, push the dirty clothing under the sheets, pull up the spread, punch out the lumps, and announce, "Hey, Mom, I've cleaned my room."

By his lights he has. It does look a lot better, and you can walk clear from the door to the far wall without tripping. What more could a mom expect?

Even so, most moms would not agree. "That room isn't cleaned." And so the debate begins.

Unless you enjoy such debating, it is better to introduce the task with a clear expectation. "I want you to clean your room Saturdays, and by cleaning your room I mean the following:

[1] Bureau and desk top clear.

[2] Toys in their box or the cupboard.

[3] Nothing under the bed.

[4] Bed made, sheets pulled up, smoothed, tucked in, same for blanket and spread.

If necessary, write him a list and stick it on the fridge door. He will protest. "Boys shouldn't have to do housework. You are making me into slave. I think I'm allergic to dust. I'll probably get sick and have to go to the hospital, and you'll probably not even bother to visit me."

Don't let him seduce you into an argument about whether you love him enough to visit him in the hospital. Stick to your agenda.

Explain the program to him. "You have until ten am when I'm coming back to check. If those four things aren't done, then I'll supervise you until they are, but if I have to supervise there'll be no cartoons for the rest of the morning."

Keep your task simple. Suppose you had included straightening his drawers, cleaning his cupboard, vacuuming the rug, taking his dirty laundry downstairs, and putting his clean clothes away. Do you think most nine-year-old boys could cope with so extensive a list? Chances are at least one item will be forgotten, so you will have to supervise and punish. You will have made the child's chance of coping a remote one, and the training will not proceed.

It is important to keep in mind that the main purpose of the discipline is not a tidy room; it is to promote the child's adaptive growth. This is more liable to happen if your program gives him a reasonable chance of success. You can always up the ante later.

So choose your expectations charitably and spell them out in unmistakable terms or else something will be missing and a debate will ensue. "Two sheets! Who needs two sheets on their bed?"1

Don't let him fudge the expectation, that is do three items and get out of the fourth with a "Gee, Mom, I did most of it." Detail your expectation charitably, then stick to all items of it.

Don't you fudge the expectations either. I know it wouldn't hurt him to move his train down to the basement while he's at it, but you should not capriciously add that item to Saturday morning room cleaning. That wasn't part of the deal, and if you do, he'll feel put upon. "Boy, give 'em and inch and they'll take a mile."

However, not all expectations are equally important. In choosing which things about which to develop disciplinary programs you should think in terms of "you must"s and "I wish you would"s.

There are things children **must** do: Get dressed. Brush their teeth. Go to school. There are other things parents wish children would do: Come to table when called. Talk politely. Be nice to your sister.

---

1   I encountered one child for whom bed making every day was just too much. He found a solution. He made his bed once —perfectly too. Then he got out his sleeping bag and from then on slept in it. Each morning he would roll it up, put it in his cupboard, and smooth the bedspread. What's a mother to do? Give him A for ingenuity and let it go. Adaptive growth is afoot.

The 'you musts' are the best areas for disciplinary programming. Children must get up and go to school and programming them to do so is wholly reasonable. Similarly children must come home on time or phone. They must do their school work. They must go to bed on time. These musts are fair game for programmed expectations.

There are things mothers wish children would do, such as wash their faces properly, comb their hair, clean their rooms, hang up their coats when they come in, or help out in the kitchen. While one can expect these things, and perhaps program some of them, it is important to keep one's priorities straight. To insist that a child wash his face properly but let him get away with not finishing his school work is to send an imbalanced message.

If one is not going to program some of the 'I wish you would's', what is one to do about them? For now, these are best handled with a shrug and, "I'll be glad when you learn to say please . . . to use your fork . . . to stop teasing your sister." Remember, you can always escalate an 'I wish you would' to a 'you must' when progress opens up the training agenda. But don't spring these changes on the child. Announce them and be prepared to defend them.

Children don't have to do everything they ought to do in order to grow up psychologically. If they do a few musts, adaptive growth will proceed. Furthermore, as growth proceeds, many of the 'I wishes' come to take care of themselves.

Summary

Set clear and reasonable expectations.
Spell these out for the child.
Stick to them.

Principle Number Two: Set a Time Limit

If you don't set a time limit by which an expectation is to be met or a task completed, you know what you will hear when you approach the child about not having taken the garbage out yet? "But

Mom, I was just gonna do it." Since you didn't set a time limit, you are not in a position to say he's failed to meet the obligation are you?

Furthermore, if you don't set a time limit, you will have to nag, and nagging is what teaches the child to ignore your words.

So, the detailed instruction becomes, "Dewey, you are to take the garbage out each afternoon before six pm. Taking the garbage out means taking this bag from this can, out that door, carrying it to that lane, depositing it in that large green receptacle with the lid, which is to be replaced, and then returning to the house and inserting a new liner in this can."

"Furthermore," the instruction continues, "the operation must be in progress by six pm sharp or else I will supervise, that is, I will find you, lead you to the trash and walk you through the details. However, since I have better things to do than supervise, that little service will cost you something."

"Even after I take the garbage out, I'm gonna get punished?"

"Yup," Mother replies, projecting a little Gary Cooper insouciance.

"You're not even gonna remind me!"

"Nope."

"But I'll forget the time."

"At first. But you'll soon learn to keep an eye on the clock."

Eventually, at two minutes to six he'll come rocketing into the kitchen, shouting, "OK! OK! I'm on my way."

So long as you are willing to get him moving, he will rely upon you to fetch him. We want to turn that job over to his conscience.

There are many ways to make sure the child has some way to know how the time is going. Most pre-school children can tell you how long until Sesame Street. The radio can be a useful reminder of an impending duty. As for the clock, one can say, "When the big hand gets to here, I'll be coming up to see if you've finished." Indeed, this kind of thing often so motivates children that learning to tell time proceeds from there.

The goal is that the child come to time himself, that instead of waiting for his mother to tell him to take out the garbage, he learns to tell himself, "It's almost six. I'd better get that garbage out." Without a time limit this internalizing growth will not proceed.

Summary

Set a time limit.
Turns parent-discipline into self-discipline.

Supervise the Task Performance

Supposing an expectation that the child take the garbage out had been communicated to him in a clear way and that a time limit of six pm had been set for the completion of the task. However, when six pm comes the garbage is still sitting there and the child is watching TV. Now what is Mother to do? She has two options.

Option One: Mother can take out the garbage herself and punish him because she had to. While this may be easier than Option Two, fetching him to the task and enduring a lot of complaint about him missing his TV, the first course of action will never solve the problem. Chances are Mother will still be taking out the garbage when he is twenty-one, after which he will marry and his wife will take over the task. 2

Trading a duty for a punishment is a trade most young children are happy to make.

Option Two: If the child is to be trained Option Two is necessary. Mother lays this out for him as follows. "Dewey, you are going to take the garbage out every night. You may do so on your own initiative, prior to six pm, and if you manage this there will be no further consequence. But, if six o'clock comes and you have not taken

2   While women, particularly those of the liberated persuasion, are much inclined to attribute male chauvinism to the inherent perversity of that other sex, the fact is male chauvinism needs to be carefully taught, and it is indulgent mothers who teach it.

the garbage out, then **I will fetch you to the task, and supervise you while you do it.** But, that will cost you, because it is your job to take out the garbage without reminders from me."

This changes the supervisory situation significantly. The action statement is no longer, "*If you don't* take the garbage out you will be punished." It has become, "*You will* take the garbage out. If you do it on your own, and by six pm, fine. If not you will be supervised to do it, but supervision will cost you something."

Given this action input, Dewey soon realizes that he cannot continue his immersion in pleasure; he must leave it one way or another. Once that becomes clear to him, the advantage of leaving it prior to punishment rather than after becomes obvious.

Even so, many mothers will select Option One, that is perform the duty for the child and punish him later. They will take out the garbage because it is easier than getting him to do it. They will pick up the child's room or alter their agenda to accommodate to him rather than hold to their expectations. They will complain bitterly of having to do his job, but they stop short of finding him, leading him to the task, supervising his performance and then punishing him for having had to supervise.

When immersed in some pleasurable activity the child is much inclined to remain in that blissful state. Faced with a choice he'll opt to avoid the duty. This does nothing for his egocentricity since he did not accommodate to Mother, she accommodated to him. Finally, such compliance from Mother is not the exercise of her rational authority that disillusions omnipotence. In fact it is the opposite, for each time Mother fails to get the child to perform the task she laid down for him, she affirms his view that he does not have to do anything he does not much feel like doing.

Supervision can be daunting. However, there is a way to go about it. Suppose the program is getting dressed in the morning. The dinger sounds. Mother goes up to supervise. Harold is stuck with the shirt buttons in the wrong holes. Mother pulls up a chair, leans back and calmyl directs operations. "Unbutton! I know it's not fair. Don't stop." He tries to persuade her it's her fault. She washed the shirt too much and the button holes shrunk. Do not respond! "Now your pants. Yes, a belt too. No, you won't throw up cause the belt's too tight."

The trick is to hang in, and keep calm. Since you left yourself time to supervise, you won't be too rushed, and since you know it's going to cost him, you don't need to punish him with your tongue. Both of those things make it easier for you to get through the job. In fifteen minutes the supervision will be over and you didn't blow up. Congratulations!

Each day you succeed it gets easier. After three or four days, when he's making it occasionally, a little faith will begin to carry you along.

George, an eight year old patient of mine came in after three weeks on a get dressed program.

"Dr Millar," he said, "you really know your job."

"That's nice to hear," I replied.

"Yep! Since you started that getting dressed program, my mother is much better."

"How so?"

"She's stopped nagging me. Now she just comes in, sits down and gives me cool dude supervision."

"Cool dude, eh!"

"Yep. Real cool! I didn't think she had it in her."

So that's how you do it, mothers. Cool dude supervision! I couldn't have said it better myself.

It can be quite difficult to supervise children through tasks. If they decide to do battle, it takes a good deal of parental assurance to stand firm. Fortunately, most children don't carry things this far. They wrangle and complain but, with Mother by their side, they perform.

However, some children dig in their heels and refuse, especially those with a real head start on the omnipotent child syndrome. They glare and shout, "I am not going to do that and you can't make me." How is Mother to supervise completion of the task under these circumstances?

There is an important truth involved here and it is best to be up front about it: **No one can make a child do that which he is absolutely determined not to do.**

This truth needs more explanation. Laws in a society and expectations in a home are the rules which make a particular social organization possible. Members benefit from their membership and they should obey the rules. If they are intelligent and mature, they come to understand this. If they do not understand, then it becomes necessary for the society to coerce such compliance. This why policemen were invented.

But laws are for people who need them. Most people don't. They do what is right, because it is right, not because it is lawful. A law cannot force a person to obey. It can jail or otherwise punish the person for not obeying, but it cannot force the person to obey. History is filled with examples of populations ignoring a bad law until society finally bandoned it. Prohibition is the first such law to come to mind.

A similar situation exists in the family. Rules can be laid down and things expected of children. But children cannot be forced to do the thing required. They can be punished but they cannot be made to conform if they are absolutely determined not to.

Though children do not yet comprehend the social contract, they do know that they have the option of refusing the task and taking the consequence. So one supervises a task, tolerates the child's complaints, waits out his resistances, weathers his stalls, and stands firm. In time most children comply.

But suppose things escalate to the point he is under the dining room table clutching the table leg and declaring that he is prepared to die under there before he takes **any** garbage into **any** lane for **anybody.**

What do you do now? Do you drag him and out and force him to do the task? Can you? I recall one father whose four year old absolutely refused to pick up his toys. Father was absolutely determined that he do so. Eventually he ended with the boy, off the floor, wedged between his knees, while Father manipulated the boy's arms as one manipulates sugar tongs. In this fashion they picked up each item one by one.

Did the father make the boy pick up his toys? Psychologically speaking, I don't think so. Would it not have been better for him to say to the boy, "All right then, I'll pick up your toys, but tomorrow they stay in the toy box, and the day after we'll see whether you've learned the rule about picking up after play is finished."

When the child absolutely refuses to conform to the supervision, it is time to back off. One makes a statement such as the following: "Of course I can't make you take out the garbage, but I may be able to make you wish you had." Then one terminates the confrontation by departing the scene.

Think about this. In dealing with the child's absolute refusal in the way that we have, are we not teaching him how democracy operates? Are we not teaching him dissent is acceptable, even defiance, if he is prepared to pay the price. When he grows up he will learn this is called civil disobedience and may eventually notice it is seen only in the democracies.

Once the parent has acknowledged the child's ultimate autonomy and, at the same time, exhibited her sensible determination, the child often capitulates, especially if the parent isn't in the room and the child's loss of face is minimized. He comes out from under the table and bumps about the room a little. Then one hears the clatter of the garbage pail accompanied by an obligatto of minimally acceptable words; "OK I'll take your dumb garbage out, Queen of the World!"

Of course, if that does happen, he still has a punishment coming because he didn't take the garbage out on time without supervision. Whatever you do, don't rub his nose in it. Just post the punishment card on the fridge and let him discover it later.

However, if, despite this best course, that doesn't happen, Mother will end having to take the garbage out herself. She should do so. In good humor!

But now he gets **two** punishments. One because he didn't take the garbage out *without* supervision, and one because he didn't take it out *with* supervision. Again it is best not to wave these under his nose.

So the third principle of discipline is, having set a clear-cut and detailed expectation, and having set a time limit for its performance, the parent deals with non-performance by finding the child, leading him to the task, and directing his performance of it. Although Mother may not succeed in this, the effort to do so will usually prove enough to get things moving and eventually accomplish the disciplinary goal, if not that day, then the next.

Summary

When the time limit is up,
And the task is incomplete,
Supervise its completion.
Cool dude is best.

So far we have dealt with the first three principles of discipline: the clear expectation, the time limit, and the supervision. It is time now to turn to the subject of the reinforcer: that measure taken to punish, reward, or otherwise induce the child to take one's disciplinary expectations seriously. It is time to grasp the nettle of punishment.

If You Had to Supervise, Apply a Reinforcer

This matter of reinforcing one's expectations is an important and complicated subject about which there is much disagreement and confusion. Let's start by being very clear about the necessity for a reinforcer.

If Dewey did not take the garbage out by six pm without Mother fetching and supervising him, it is necessary that some consequence ensue. This could be a scolding, a punishment, or a reward withheld. If there is no such consequence, why should he move on the task until his mother arrives to make him? Why should he not just sit enjoying his show, hoping that perhaps this once she will give up and he won't have to do it? He has nothing to lose and a minuscule hope of gain.

If the child is to come to accept an expectation, his failure to do so without supervision has to cost him something. Mother has to lay something like this on the child.

"Dewey! Because you did not take out the garbage by six o'clock, you will not be allowed to ride your bike after school tomorrow, and that's the way it is going to be each day until you learn to watch the clock and get the garbage out by six."

The function of the reinforcer is to lead the child to discipline himself. If one only fetches him to the undone task and supervises his completion of it but does not apply a reinforcer, one will be fetching and supervising forever.

If supervision is invariably accompanied by a reinforcer, eventually he will be skittering out before the deadline in order to meet the expectation and avoid the consequence. This does not have to happen very many times before adaptive growth is in motion.

What exactly is a reinforcer? A reinforcer is a parental action undertaken to lend weight to her disciplinary expectations. The reinforcer empowers the disciplinary communication. Children immersed in pleasure do not hear a parental summons or prohibition. However, as was illustrated with the Second Telling Program in Chapter 3, once they realize that if they do not respond some consequence will result, their hearing improves. The consequence served to reinforce the communication.

Reinforcers come in two varieties: those whose power comes from approval and those whose power emanates from disapproval. Approval ranges from smiles and praise to tangible rewards. Disapproval ranges from frowns and scoldings to punishments. Each of these has its place in parenting.

Though it is much more pleasant for the parent to approve than to disapprove, as we shall see later, approval is not always effective, particularly with the toddler who has as yet little awareness of the fact that his mother is not required by God to approve him on all occasions regardless of his behavior.

So, having put things in context, let's now address ourselves to understanding the most essential of reinforcers, punishment.

Punishent as Reinforcer

Punishment is a consequence contrived by the parent to disreward some unacceptable behavior. It is a perfectly respectable part of parenthood. Unfortunately the **noun** punishment has become confused with the **adjective** punitive, which means cruel or mean forms of punishment, undertaken by sadistic persons for its own sake.

So it has come to be that when one recommends even reasonable punishments, there are those who think you have an unhealthy desire to hurt children. This nonsense has been popularized to the point that many parents have been frightened away from their disciplinary responsibilities. This has made a substantial contribution to the escalating incidence of omnipotent children in our homes and schools.

Since parents must understand when and how to punish as part of their parenting, let's spend a few minutes making sure we know what the word means. According to Webster, to punish is to "afflict with pain, loss or suffering for a crime or fault: to chasten."

Webster lists as synonyms, "chastise, castigate, chasten, discipline, correct."

When it comes to parents dealing with children, let me spell out exactly what is going on when a punishment is administered.

SOMEONE (the parent) does SOMETHING (the punishment, unwelcome but not unreasonable) to the OFFENDER (the child) with a view to PENALIZING (that is devaluing and retributing) as well as CORRECTING (altering through psychological means) the unacceptable behavior.

The most convenient and effective punishment for training children is the removal of a privilege. Here are some examples.

"Because you did not take out the garbage by seven, without supervision, you will not be allowed to watch TV between seven and seven-thirty tonight."

"Because you did not finish dressing by seven-fifty this morning, without supervision, you will not be allowed to ride your bike after school today."

"Because you did not get to bed on time tonight, without supervision, I will not play a card game with you tomorrow night after supper."

The removal of a privilege is a much better punishment than assigning an extra duty, mostly because the consequence is easier to administer. Telling the child, "Because you did not take the garbage out, without supervision, you will have to put the dishes away," involves you in supervising putting the dishes away. If the child is angry and determined, you could end punishing for not cooperating in a punishment. Now there's a slippery slope its best not to venture upon.

People sometimes complain that their child has no privileges to remove. In these days of many privileged children this is rarely true. Their definition of privilege is different from mine. They will say, for example, "Oh no, I can't take away any of his playtime. Children have a right to playtime." Playtime is a right?

I certainly agree one ought not to remove a child's rights as punishment, so his meals (not desserts) should be sacrosanct, as should his home (no child should be turfed out of the house as punishment), and his bed (no child should be made to sleep on the floor). However, I do not believe a bicycle, unlimited playtime, or TV cartoons are among the inalienable rights of childhood.

People are sometimes despairing about punishment because it does not seem to bother the child. The fact is, any child can find something reasonably pleasant do when denied TV for half an hour, or his bicycle fro an afternoon. Some days he doesn't ride his bike after school. Obviously losing a half an hour of TV or an afternoon's use of his bicycle is not going to cause the child major distress. "So," they say, "what's the use of a punishment that doesn't hurt?"

Then, they may pile on the punishment in the hope that a large enough dose will hurt. This is a losing game. The parent ends up assigning a hopelessly excessive punishment, which they then have to recant while guess-who stands there grinning snidely.

It is very hard to help young parents understand that, in order to be effective, a punishment does not have to *hurt* the child. However, the impact of punishment is ninety percent psychological. It is important for parents to understand this so let me spend a little time clarifying the psychology of punishment.

Let's begin with an illustration from my practice. This kind of situation sometimes develops in my playroom. A six or seven year old begins to see me regularly, usually because his mother is having trouble getting him to mind. I visit with him in my playroom, where we talk, draw pictures and play games. Gradually, as he becomes secure in my setting, he starts acting with me in the way he acts at home. That is to say he messes about a little.

"It's time to pick up the block game," I say, as the clock nears the hour.

"Nope," he says, if he responds at all.

"Come on," I say. "You have to help."

"Too tired," he says.

" That's the rule. If you play with a game, you have to help put it away."

"Not gonna."

Since I have been around this particular maypole a few times , I don't try to make him. I say, "Well, OK. If you won't pick them up I will, but that means you can't play with this game next week."

He gives me a look, shrugs his shoulders, looks over at my shelf full of games and says, "Who cares? I'll play with sumpin' else."

After I finish picking up the pieces, I write a little note on a scrap of paper, saying the words aloud as I write them. "Johnny can't play with this game next week." I stick it to the front of the game box with a piece of Scotch tape. As I am doing so, he watches me closely, but looks away when he catches my eye.

When he leaves, I open my appointment book to next week and write *game* under his name. That's so I won't forget about the punishment I've administered.

The next week when he arrives, I see my note, go into the playroom and remove the game in question. I deposit it in the secretary's office before I bring him in.

Although it's been a week, and he's only seven years old, and there's a whole shelf of other games, I see his eyes searching the playroom, looking for that game. If he doesn't care, as he said, why is he looking?

I don't say anything. I know from experience he will eventually ask me. He doesn't want to, because he has already said he doesn't care, but there is something else gnawing at him. He doesn't want me to get away with punishing him.

Finally he can stand it no longer. "Where's that . . . ah, block game?" he asks in a elaborately casual manner.

"Don't you remember? You're not allowed to play with that because you wouldn't help pick it up last time."

"I don't care! I don't care about the dumb block game!" he says. But it is clear from his pursed mouth and angry eyes that he does care. Miffed, he looks around for something not quite acceptable to do. One thing most children his age eventually hit on is my children's sink. He walks over, turns the water on, and with a little calculated carelessness spills some water on my rug.

"Turn the water off, you're splashing," I say. But he doesn't and some more splashes on my rug.

After many years of practice, I have equipped my playroom to handle this kind of thing. The cabinet below my sink unlocks. I reach in and turn off the water taps from within. Then I close the door and lock it again. Now when he turns the taps, no water comes out.

"Turn the water on," he says.

"No," I reply. "You splash."

"I won't splash."

"You might," I reply. "Today we'll play with something else. Next week when you come again, you can try the sink and we'll see if you've learned not to splash."

At this point he will either have a tantrum or sulk a while. Either way eventually he will settle down. Most likely we will get involved in some other game. Now when it comes time to pick up the pieces and put them away, he helps.

But you know what this kind of child always does? Leave one last piece not picked up. That's to prove he really didn't obey. Omnipotence does not give up without a struggle. Since, he has come so far my way, I guess I can let him save a little face. I pick up that last piece and put it in the box for him.

"You missed this one," I say.

What's going on here? There are lots of toys in my playroom. He could have played with something else. The real pain of losing the block game was minimal. But the psychological impact was such that he was bothered enough about the loss to remember a whole week and react when reminded of his deprivation. Something was bothering him. If not the pain of losing the game then what?

What bothers a child in such a situation is not that he loses the game, or the half hour TV, or the bicycle. It's that you had *the nerve to punish him.* The punishment is a statement of your authority and this shakes up his omnipotence illusion.

Here's a thing children often do to deal with this. They invoke the "sweet lemon" gambit. The child deprived of his bicycle after school because he did not dress without supervision says blithely, "As a matter of fact, I wasn't planning to ride my bike after school." And, when the time comes, he cheerfully finds something else to do.

Had the parent removed a TV show, the reaction would have been the same. With the sweet lemon the child is seeking to deny the parent's power to punish him. That he goes to the trouble to do this suggests that something is bothering him.

We know what now, don't we?

If the parent, understanding that the child is simply trying to deny her power to punish, blithely replies, "That's all right. If you were planning to ride your bike, you wouldn't be allowed," the child will be surprised, perhaps even shocked. The sweet lemon is supposed to disarm. It seems not to have done so. She doesn't care!

He may change his tune and protest that it's his bike and she has no right to steal it, even for an afternoon. He may not, but after a few such occasions, the sweet lemon gambit loses its power.

Here is another example that makes my point about the essentially psychological impact of punishment. A mother, misunderstanding a detail of my punishment cards system allowed her child to choose his own card. Blindly! She laid the cards face down on the table, and let him pick one.

The card he picked said, "No cat in with you at bedtime tonight." She was dismayed with the card that had turned up for she had intended removing that card because he hadn't bothered with the cat for the last two weeks. Obviously the punishment would be meaningless to him. It was not.

"Not that!" her child wailed. "Take TV! Take my bike! Anything but my cat!"

You see how it works? Once losing the cat at bedtime was defined as a a punishment the loss became psychologically significant, and he reacted to it. If she had chosen it, he might have given here the sweet lemon, but having chosen it himself, he could hardly be thumbing his nose at her punishment, could he?

Yousee? Its not the loss of pleasure that counts, it's that you had the nerve to punish him.

There are a few really clever kids who find ways to play the sweet lemon game that are truly impressive.

Remember when Aunt Polly punished Tom Sawyer by requiring that he whitewash the fence on Saturday morning instead of going fishing? At first Tom was devastated, but then the natural psychologist in him took over.

When his friends passed by on their way to fishing he barely noticed them, he was so engrossed in the pleasures of whitewashing. It took them some time for them to appreciate that Tom was enjoying himself, that the privilege of whitewashing fences was a joy that seldom came his way, and he was making the most of it.

With studied reluctance Tom allowed each boy to *purchase* a fragment of the job. In time, Tom was reclined on the grass, surrounded by his loot, supervising his eager gang of fence artists. Through the alchemy of applied psychology he had converted Aunt Polly's punishment into a coveted reward. But did he not know, in his heart, that he was only kidding himself with his variation on the sweet lemon gambit?

The function of punishment is communication. It is action dia logue. It says to the child more clearly and more penetratingly than words that he is a child with a child's prerogatives in a world where many of the decisions are made by adults. Punishment requires the child to accept his childhood at the same time as he accepts his parents' authority.

Since the pain of punishment is less important than its psychological content, a mild punishment has the same communicative value as a severe one. Thus the mild is to be preferred.

Why? For three reasons. In the first place it is *kinder*. In the second it is *less productive of parental guilt*, and, finally, it is *more manageable*.

If you have to punish frequently, as you must when retraining omnipotent children, with mild punishments it is possible do so. However, if one removes the TV for a week at a time, one will soon have removed it until he is thirteen or entering high school, whichever comes first, and that is a game no one can play for long.

In my experience, the best punishments are the removal of privileges since they are easiest supervised. Next comes the assignment of chores or extra duties. As I have said, the trouble with these is that you have to supervise their completion, and that can lead to more struggle and more punishment. The third and final method is corporal punishment, a euphemism for spanking.

In my view, spanking has a minimal role to play in child rearing. If it is used sparingly in the pre-school child, it retains its dramatic impact. The four year old who runs out on the street and makes a face at the passing cars needs an impressive statement of wrongdoing. However, if parents use spanking too much it loses its here and now effectiveness.

For grade-school children spanking is not as effective a reinforcer as a planned privilege removal. However, there are situations where it is not wholly inappropriate. In my play, *Don't Shoot, I'm Your Mother,* Lydia tolerates a lot more from Dewey than she ought, but when he finally spits in her face, she decides enough is enough.

Summary

Punishment is psychological.
Its function is communication.
Mild is better.

Punishment Cards

There is a system I have devised which helps weak parents to stick to their guns, and angry parents to stay in bounds. I published this in a paper entitled *A Card A Day Keeps The Social Worker Away.*[3] It begins with a list of privilege losses.

Lose half an hour prime-time TV
Lose half an hour Nintendo
Lose bike privilege for one day
Lose half an hour outside play time
Lose Lego for one day
Lose Cabbage Patch for one day
No friend over this week
No visit to friend's house this week
Lose telephone privileges for one day
No game with Mom or Dad today
No story after supper
Lose half on hour Saturday cartoons

3   B.C. Medical Journal 29, No. 11 (November 1987). Permission is gratefully acknowledged.

Of course each family will have its own special privilege activities suitable for use as punishments.

One inscribes each of these on a card. Use your imagination. For pre-schoolers you can draw a picture of big bird which means he loses Sesame street. Each loss is quantified; lose half an hour TV, or, if it works better, no TV after school is card one, no TV after supper is card two, lose bike for one day, card three. Try to get about eight cards. Make a duplicate set, in case these first set disappears. Now put all the cards in a box labeled Punishment Cards and put it in plain sight.

Notice that none of these is mean. None amounts to a serious deprivation. Note also, the child's **rights** are not involved, only his or her **privileges.**

Since parents are going to have to punish the child as part of his adaptive training, it is a good idea to be ready to do so - hence the cards. If you aren't prepared it is easy to overshoot the mark, like taking away TV for a week and then having to recant, or to let the punishment go because you're just too tired to think of anything right now, and later you forget about it. Inconsistency of this kind doesn't train.

Tell him, "If you earn a punishment I will choose one of these cards and post it on the fridge where it will stay until the punishment is served, and then it will go back in the box for future use."

You can post the card in the morning, and, even though the punishment doesn't come up until after school, you have connected the consequence to the offence.

Here's an interesting thing. When you post the card, the child will protest. Almost never do you hear the sweet lemon. Then when it comes time to serve the punishment, he takes it without protest. Indeed some children will remind their mothers when they come home from school. "Remember Mom, I don't get cartoons today."

What we have done is separate the act of punishing from the consequence or privilege loss and seen that the child reacts more to getting the card than the actual punishment. Does this not demonstrate the psychological reality I have been talking about.

Another advantage of punishment cards is that, for little children of five, six, and seven, cards are a lot more real than words. "You'll get a punishment" is vague; "You'll get a card from your box" initiates a concrete sequence the child soon comes to understand and believe in. Even if he has to wait an hour until you get around to selecting the card.

It is a good idea to guard your cards, perhaps even make a duplicate set, in case the first disappear.

Programming a routine like getting dressed in the morning is easy with a box of cards from which to select a consequence if the child doesn't make it on time without supervision. Once this, the heaviest aspect of discipline, is organized, the process becomes a piece of cake.

Reward as Reinforcer

Reward, that is providing some good thing for behavior which meets the parent's expectation, seems on the surface to be the converse of punishment. It is not. It is quite different.

As action dialogue, reward makes a different statement. Punishment says, "If you don't do this by this time you will be punished." With reward the statement becomes, "If you do this by this time, you will receive a reward."

Because the statement is positive in tone, and the contract a giving one, many parents find the idea of reward as a reinforcer more palatable than punishment. However, the psychological impact of reward is significantly different. Before clarifying those differences, let me put the matter into a life context.

Supposing we were to set up the same training program for getting dressed in the morning such as was discussed earlier in this book, but, instead of using punishment as a reinforcer, we used reward.

Now the communication to the child would go something like this: "Tommy, I want you to get dressed in the morning. That means all your clothes, including underwear and socks, buttons in the right holes, and shoes tied. You have until eight am. I won't remind you, but I will put the clock in your room so you will know when the time is up."

To this point the instructions are identical whether performance is to be rewarded or non-performance punished. However, if reward is to be the mode of reinforcement, Mother says, "Tommy, if when I come up at eight, you have finished dressing, I will reward you. I will add five cents to your allowance this week. "If," Mother continues, "you are not dressed, I will supervise your dressing, but then there will be no reward."

Since Tommy has been having his troubles getting dressed in the morning, the chances are his limitation in patience will still let him down when the sock sticks or the buttons get into the wrong holes. So he won't make it those first few mornings, and it will be necessary to withhold the reward.

Tommy did not dress and he was not rewarded. How has his situation changed? Not at all. He was not dressing before, he is not dressing now. An actual reward has not entered the picture, only the promise of one. There has been no change in his reality situation, as there would have been had punishment been the chosen reinforcer.

What does not receiving a reward say to Tommy? Nothing! No action dialogue has taken place. The only message Tommy received was the verbal one with which Mother began the program. In essence this came down to, "You may dress on time if you wish, and I would prefer that you do so, and, if you do, you will receive a benefit, but if you do not, I will supervise as before and nothing more will happen."

Big whoop de doo!

The fact is non-reward speaks in such a soft voice that it may not be register with the immature child.

Consider the same program using punishment as a reinforcer. This time mother will conclude her instruction as follows, "If you aren't dressed when I come up at eight o'clock, I will supervise you, but since I have better things to do with my time, I will punish you. Every morning that I have to supervise, you will lose your TV privilege between seven-thirty and eight that evening. And that is the way it will be until you have learned to dress yourself on time and without my supervising you."

Now if Tommy fails to perform he receives his punishment and his situation changes. He loses half an hour of TV. While he may deny that this concerns him, there is no question that his circumstances have changed as a consequence of his failure to perform without supervision. Unlike reward, punishment speaks in a voice that a child can only pretend not to hear.

There is a more important consideration with respect to adaptive growth involved here. As I have said repeatedly throughout this book, punishment makes a psychological statement that is essential to promoting the child's adaptive growth. Punishment defines the child as a child and the adult as an adult. **Punishment challenges the child's omnipotence illusion.** It is this challenge that the child cannot ignore and which generates adaptive growth.

Reward issues no such challenge. Reward does not say "You must". It says, "If you will, you will benefit." It implies that the child does not have to do as the parent wishes unless he chooses to. **So it is that reward panders to the omnipotence illusion.** This is the what makes reward so much less effective in promoting adaptive growth.

Training programs reinforced by reward tend to be unsuccessful. The child continues to do as he always has done and quickly reconciles himself to the loss of the promised reward. And then where can the parent go except to a fresh program, this time utilizing punishment as a reinforcer?

· Let us, just for the sake of demonstration, assume that, despite its weak voice, reward did induce some little money grubber to get dressed on time. Each morning he dresses; each evening he is rewarded. After three weeks he is getting an extra five cents per day added to his allowance.

What now? Is the parent to go on rewarding the child forever? Thirty-five cents! It's probably worth it. Except for one thing. Parents begin to ask themselves, 'Should I be paying this child to do what every other child on the street does without getting paid?'

Eventually the parent will decide to terminate rewarding. Can she? Will the child now regress to not dressing again?

When punishment works, the reinforcer disappears from the equation. When reward works, it stays on stage. Soon it becomes a problem. Furthermore, reward teaches children to greet each new expectation with "What will you give me if I do it?"

Psychologically speaking, reward is not the converse of punishment. It is something very different. It has its uses, but these are not prominent when remedial parenting is the name of the game.

Here, in tabular form, is a summary of the differences between reward and punishment as a reinforcer of discipline.

PUNISHMENT	REWARD
Communicates loudly	Communicates softly
Disullusions omnipotence	Panders to omnipotence
Disappears with improvement	Remains with improvement
Hard to do	Easy to do

Other Approaches

Many parents would like to avoid the whole disciplinary exchange. As adults dealing with one another they depend upon reason to persuade others to modify their behavior. It is civilized and a lot more pleasant than having to get into all this expecting and reinforcing. So they talk to their children rather than discipline them.

Not infrequently I hear of parents getting into exchanges with toddlers like this. "If you spill that on my rug," Mother *explains* to her two year old who has somehow gotten hold of a bottle of ink, "it will cause a stain. Stains are hard to get out. Mother will have to work very hard, on her hands and knees, to try to get it out. And if that doesn't work Daddy will have to call the rug cleaners and pay them lots of money, and Daddy has to work hard for the money. Now you don't want Daddy and Mommy to have to work hard do you?"

While the child may be solemnly attentive while Mother goes through this account, his response will often reveal how little of Mother's monologue actually penetrated his awareness. "How did the stains get into the bottle? Never mind! I'll let them out. Whoopee! Stains all out."

The more civilized and educated the parents are, the more liable they are to fall into this error. Because they depend so much on words to choose and govern their own behavior, and it is so long since they were a child, they forget how toddlers think. So they explain, and expect their explanation to persuade the child.

If your dog wet on the rug would you get down on your hands and knees and explain to him? "You know if you didn't wet on the rug, the room would smell a lot nicer. And I'd like you better. Who knows, you might even like yourself better."

You don't reason with dogs. What you do is some variant of the following. Push his nose down to the wet, whap him on the head with a rolled up newspaper, and lead him to his box in the corner. A certain amount of this action dialogue and it will occur to the dog, "If I go directly to the box I can avoid that whap on the head." And so he does.

Of course children are not dogs. The toddler has some language. Even so, verbal communication is new in his life. For him, action dialogue is still the main mode of communication. One hopes, in time, words will mean more to him. For now, explaining is 'talking to the dog.'

In my example, Mother would have been better to explain less, emit a little emotion, and move fast. "Hand me that ink bottle this instant or you will find yourself in your bed." If the child gets the message in time, chances are it will the tone in mother's voice that impresses him, not the words.

There are two methods of reinforcer which, being verbal in char acter, become more useful as the child grows older. These are approval and disapproval.

For **Approval - disapproval** , that is communicating pleasure or displeasure with respect to the child's behavior, to work a number of prior conditions must be present.

For a child to want to gain his parents approval, that is please her, he must be able to perceive that his parent is sometimes pleased and other times displeased. So, a degree of adaptive maturity with respect to egocentricity must have been established before approval can be an effective reinforcer. In egocentric, omnipotent children the child's awareness of others is such that approval-disapproval is minimally effective.

The second essential condition for approval/disapproval to modify behavior comes into play after that level of necessary interpersonal awareness has been reached. Once the child is able to perceive his parent's pleasure or displeasure, he must come to see that these parental reactions are related, in some consistent way, to his behavior.

Capricious disapproval, heard only when Mother 'has had it up to here,' cannot train because the child sees it as related to his mother's annoyance not his behavior. Undeserved disapproval weakens the system.

Similarly, expressions of approval uttered because the mother is feeling badly about her child's self-esteem and wants to praise him only weaken praise as a reinforcer. Undeserved praise also weakens that system.

Even so, many child rearing books are forever advising parents to 'try to find something to praise in his behavior.' My advice, "If you have to look for something to praise, don't bother. When you really feel pleased with him, you will show it, and he will know it."

There is a third condition essential to the effective use of approval-disapproval as a reinforcer of discipline. There must be a reasonable reservoir of good will between parent and child.

In the case history which began this book Dewey's mother had reached the point that she was crosswise with Dewey a good deal of the time. Good will between them had been steadily eroded, and disapproval was almost constant. For Dewey, being in the psychological soup had become a way of life. He and his mother had become mired in profitless displeasure with one another.

Why would a child modify his behavior to gain his mother's approval when he can barely remember what approval felt like? How can his mother offer approval when most of the time he is so provocative that she can barely stand being with him?

While it's possible that approval-disapproval will some day replace punishment as Mother's mode of dealing with Dewey, it won't be before some good will has been restored to their relationship.

This can only happen one way. Dewey has to become more lovable and then his mother can come to feel more loving towards him. Punishment can get them there. Let me illustrate.

Let's recall our program for getting dressed in the morning. We set up the expectation and the time limit. We had supervised if necessary and, if we had to, given Dewey a punishment. Dewey was soon dressing more mornings than not and getting fewer punishments.

Now, since Dewey has been getting ready on time most mornings, he and Mother don't start each day cross at each other. Some mornings are actually pleasant. They have time to visit over breakfast, and they aren't constantly annoyed with each other. A little good will has re-entered their relationship.

Supposing one morning Dewey does something to annoy his mother, and Mother shows her annoyance. Perhaps she becomes a little disapproving or scolds. It's possible that Dewey, who has been enjoying the good will too, will raise his hands and exclaim, "OK! OK! I'll do it. Don't get mad."

Because amity has been restored between them, Dewey is now impressed by her disapproval and modifies his behavior to make things right between them. Approval-disapproval is on the way to becoming a useful form of disciplinary reinforcement. In time Mother will have less and less need to resort to punishment as reinforcer.

In summary then, approval-disapproval is an effective mode of disciplinary reinforcement when the child is mature enough to perceive his parent's state of feeling, and when a reasonable reservoir of good will exists between the parent and child. However, for the very young child, or the child in difficulties with his adaptive growth, approval-disapproval tends to be ineffective.

A Popular Pseudo-reinforcer

Before leaving the subject of disciplinary reinforcers, there is a popular strategy which ought to be discussed briefly. It is called *natural consequences*. Many parents find it a most attractive notion.

It goes something like this. If the child fails to perform some expectation, or ignores some disciplinary limit, the parent does not punish him. The parent allows the *natural consequence* of the child's behavior to develop, and that punishes the child.

If the child dawdles over dressing, the parent ignores the dawdling and allows the child to be late for school. You see, being late to school is the natural consequence of dawdling over dressing. That will teach him!

While other advantages are sometimes cited, I believe the appeal of natural consequences is that it allows the parent to avoid the painful task of punishing the child. The parent does not have to feel guilty for denying the child or visiting some unpleasure upon him. This gets the parent off the disciplinary hook. It says, from mother to child, "Don't blame me. It wasn't I who punished you; it was the world."

For the omnipotent child such a maternal cop-out confirms his omnipotence. "You see. She isn't the boss of me. She has no right to punish me and she knows it."

Natural consequences operate for the benefit of the parent not the child.

A natural consequence does not have the psychological effect of a reinforcer. It doesn't assist with the training.

Furthermore it is very often quite unrealistic. Consider the following questions and you will readily see what I mean.

If the child is too young to perceive the consequence of his action, is it fair to allow him to proceed and suffer that consequence?

If the mother allows the child to dawdle and as a consequence be late for school, is she not shifting the responsibility for punishing the child on to the shoulders of the teacher? What if the teacher believes in natural consequences and ignores the child's lateness, saying, "The natural consequence of being late every morning is missing half of math class, the natural consequence of which is eventually to fail math?" Is not this natural consequence so remote from getting dressed in the morning that it has no hope of every modifying that behavior? Is it fair to the child to let him fail?

Furthermore, there are many behaviors for which no natural consequence exists.4 Things like beating up younger brother who can't fight back. What about being rude to Mother?Unless mother invents a consequence, the behavior goes unchecked. There is a natural consequence, in time mother hates to see arrive home from school.

Also, there are many other natural consequences that are wholly unacceptable, some a dereliction of the parent's duty to protect the child, such as getting cavities because one allows the child not to brush his teeth.

The most damaging effect of the natural consequence notion, however, is that it seduces parents into abdicating their duty to disillusion the child's omnipotence and lead him into a reasonable acceptance and comfort in the true limitations of his personal power. Children need to make their peace with authority, to give up their willful desire to make all decisions, to accept limits, but at the same time not to become so cowed that they cannot stand up for their rights as individuals. They need to find their way to a sense of autonomy, that is a sense of their right and capacity to become self- determining individuals within the structures of society and humanity.

---

4   For such cases there is a companion program, *logical consequences*. If the child hits his sister, mother hits him. If the child bites, mother bites him. A little primitive, this logic, isn't it?

Children achieve such autonomy by working through their relation to authority. This is best accomplished in that *safe battling between the child and his parents*. However, if the parents decline to engage in that battle, if they abdicate their authority and hide behind natural consequences, this working through cannot take place. When it does not the child is not led to surrender his omnipotence illusion and he remains adaptively immature. Now is he in danger of becoming an omnipotent child who must fly in the face of community expectations, protest for the sake of protesting, and reject all rules as personal affronts.

Children are not well-served when parents abdicate their responsibility to discipline. Parenting systems which talk of the parent-child interaction as a 'relationship of equals' confuse parents and foster such abdication. Such systems are not part of the solution; they are part of the problem.

So far, in our discussion of the principles of discipline, we have learned how to *define expectations and limits clearly*. We have come to understand how the *time limit* leads the child toward *self-supervision*. We have seen how supervising the expectation and applying some kind of a *consequence* because supervision was necessary are essential if adaptive growth is to result. It is time now to deal with the fifth and final principle of discipline, the need to persist.

Persist to Train

It is rarely the case that children will modify their behavior promptly and permanently simply because the parent tells them to do so or punishes them once or twice for non-compliance. Parents sometimes think this should happen, and when it doesn't they wonder if the punishment was perhaps not impressive enough. Many parents seek that single dramatic action that will so impress the child that "He will never do that again."

Here are a few examples. Mother washes his mouth out with soap so that he will never swear again. Dad makes him smoke a cigar to teach him never to smoke again. Mother bites the child, to teach him not to bite others.

To be fair, these single dramatic actions sometimes work, but they often don't. I

Spanking is one such dramatic input. If used only on rare occasions, it can be useful with the pre-school child. If he dumps your aspidistra in the middle of the ivory rug, a whack on the bottom may be the right medicine. If his mother is not in the habit of whacking, this dramatic input may well abolish such decorative impulses.

However, the best training results from persistent application of soundly designed disciplinary inputs. It takes time to change behavior and time for that behavior change to generate growth and change attitudes. The best way to illustrate the role of persistence in discipline is to describe the usual course of events when one undertakes a program of retraining a child who is lagging in some area of adaptive growth.

Supposing Mother has decided to make sure Trevor gets to bed on time, not simply because this is an area of tension between them but also because she wants to promote his adaptive growth. Let's have her apply the principles of discipline.

The first thing she does is set a clear expectation. "Trevor," she says, "every night I have to tell you two or three times to get ready for bed. You always say 'inna minute' and I have to get cross and chase you into the bathroom to brush your teeth. I am tired of doing this, so from now on we are going to have a getting-to-bed-on-time program."

"Ya mean you're not gonna nag me anymore? Hooray!"

"That's right. From now on I expect you to get into your pajamas, brush your teeth, wash your face and be ready for me to tuck you in without me reminding or nagging." At this juncture she shows him the timer.

She now explains the time limit. "See this Trevor. This is your timer. At eight I am setting it for fifteen minutes and that is how long you have to do all the things I expect."

"But that means my bedtime will be eight-fifteen. There isn't a kid on the block has to go to bed at eight-fifteen."

"Eight-thirty," Mother says. "I'm allowing fifteen minutes for me to supervise if I have to. And don't give me that 'too early' garbage. Eight-fifteen I expect you to be ready."

"Whattya mean supervise? I know how to put on my pajamas."

"I know you do, so do it. And the rest! If you don't finish before the timer goes off, you will have my company until you do."

If at eight-fifteen, when the dinger sounds, she finds Trevor still watching TV or on his way to the bathroom. She leads him the rest of the way through the routine, standing by while he puts on his pajamas, taking him to the bathroom to brush his teeth, whatever on the list is still undone.

As she does this she tries her best to keep her cool, not yell or scold, just supervise. And because she has a plan she manages to contain herself. She tucks him in. It may be eight-thirty by now, perhaps even later, but he's in.

Now she moves to step four. She applies a reinforcer. "Because I had to supervise you tonight, Trevor, tomorrow night you lose your TV from seven-thirty to eight."

"You mean I have to go to bed early!"

"Oh no, your bedtime doesn't change. You can do what you like with the half hour, except that you can't watch TV. That's your punishment."

"Don't you know punishment is mean?"

"Not this one."

"It's your fault I was late. You didn't remind me."

"It's not my job to remind you. It's your job to keep an eye on your timer."

"I don't care about your dumb punishment. As a matter of fact, I wasn't planning to watch TV tomorrow night."

Noting the scent of lemon in the air, Mother smiles, "Well, if you were, you wouldn't be allowed to."

Now Mother comes to the part where fortitude is required. She persists. While occasionally the child will respond to Mother's clear enunciation of expectations with prompt compliance, typically, for the first three nights Trevor doesn't make it, is supervised, and the reinforcer is applied. The first two times he is blithe about his punishment, but the third he changes his tune. "You're mean. That's my favorite show. Kids got a right to TV. I'm calling the child abuse line."

The fourth and fifth days he makes it and does not need to be punished. Now, because there have been no consequences for two days, he forgets all about the program, and on day six when Mother comes back after setting his timer, she finds him glued to the box.

At this point, many parents give up. "The program didn't work," they say, and decide to try something else.

What did they expect, magic?

What they should do is continue in exactly the same pattern of supervision and punishment. After two more days of punishment, he gets moving again. This time the improvement lasts for four days before he slips back once more.

If one were to graph copings vs punishments administered one would find the former rising and the latter falling. Even so, it takes a good four weeks for a turn around to be clearly established. This is why persistence is such an important aspect of discipline.

Parents must understand that they are engaged in teaching the child and that adaptive learning depends upon repetition. They must not lose sight of the fact that the goal of the program is not simply behavior change, i.e. getting the child to bed on time. It is to promote adaptive growth.

What we are trying to do is stretch the child's tolerance for tedium, require him to become less egocentric, persuade him to accommodate to others, and lead him away from omnipotence. We are more interested in these things than in the amount of sleep he gets.

Once the parent grasps this, it will become clear that learning proceeds not only on those days when he makes it to bed without having to be punished but also on those days when he requires punishment.

The learning, of course, is different when he makes it than when he doesn't.

When he makes it, he *exercises a little patience and persistence* and stretches that adaptive competency. Furthermore, he copes, which does something for his *self-esteem.*

When he doesn't make it, is supervised and the reinforcer applied, his mother has intruded upon his *egocentricity*, which not only teaches him to accommodate but also challenges his *omnipotence illusion.*

So when Trevor makes it, Mother wins something, and when he doesn't make it, Mother wins something else. And either way, in the long run Trevor wins.

One usually finds that in four weeks the child is getting to bed on time without supervision six nights out of seven. But you cannot stop the program yet. If you do, in another four weeks you'll be back to square one. Indeed, you cannot even be flexible yet. If you alter the bedtime **one** night, because there is a special TV show he has got to see, you can be sure the next night he will wail, "But you let me stay up last night."

Children in adaptive training regard parent flexibility as weakness, not consideration, and they try it on the next night. So parents must hold firm, greeting each deviation from the pattern as cause for supervision and reinforcement, remembering that it takes two ,or even three, months for external or parental expectations to become internal or self- expectations.

This is the psychological process one is setting in motion, teaching the child to make his parents' expectations his own, leading him to the point that an inner voice will be telling him what to do rather than the outer voice of his parents. Persistence provides the time for this process of internalization to take place. Eventually the habit takes and a sense of **ought to** begins to form in the child's mind.

He is beginning to accept that it is his obligation to get into bed on time. Soon he is boasting of it. "Hey, Mom. Notice how I'm always ready when is time to tuck me in. How about that, eh?" What you're also hearing in that comment is a building block of self-esteem settling firmly into place.

When one programs discipline, the psychological changes follow in this order.

Behavior changes first.

Then one sees evidence of **adaptive growth** i.e. signs of a little more self-control, a little more consideration, a growing tendency to go off grumbling rather than to challenge or defy.

Finally, **attitudes change.** He no longer feels so put-down by expectations and is less prideful now that he no longer sees them as an infringement on his right to be wholly self-determining.

Persistence is as crucial a principle of discipline as the other four. Unless disciplinary programs are persisted in firmly and without significant variation for at least a six weeks, and be clearly in the wings for use when necessary for the next two months, the training will not accomplish all that it can. There is one comfort; the longer you persist, the easier it gets.

We have now examined the five principles of discipline in detail. Looking back at the problem from this new perspective it all seems quite straightforward, doesn't it? Even so, there are many omnipotent children out there. Can these be children be remedially parented or is it too late?

It has been my experience that most pre-adolescent children can be retrained. The younger they are, the easier the training is to manage. Even so, it's a challenging endeavor and the parents have to do all the work. But, if they are willing to extend themselves, there's a very good chance remedial parenting will work.

In the next , and final, chapter I plan to show you how I design an overall program of remedial parenting.

8

Remedial Parenting

The first chapters of this book have been concerned with the fundamentals of adaptive growth in children. It's time to convert these fundamentals into a program for a school age child in difficulties with his growing up. I call this remedial parenting.

To prevent a child becoming an omnipotent child is easier than leading a child deep into the syndrome back to normal growth, and the approach is different. It is for this reason that I have decided to limit *The Omnipotent Child III* to remediating the school age child, and to write another book dealing with training in the pre-school years.

I believe the best approach to describing a program of remedial parenting is to tell you how I would have started Lydia and Frank getting Dewey back on track.

In Chapter 1 I recorded the facts obtained through my history taking and my interview with Dewey. Here is what happens next. After making a treatment plan, I arrange to see Lydia and Frank to give them my findings. Dewey is not invited, of course.

"When I told him we were coming," Frank said, holding Lydia's chair for her, "he wanted to know when he was coming back." Frank raised his eyebrows. "Kinda surprised me. The way he barreled out of here I was sure this was the last place he'd ever want to come back to."

"I hope he wasn't too difficult," Lydia said, starting to mangle her gloves again.

"We had a lively time. He's a sharp boy."

"He said he liked you," Frank said.

"Even when they storm out, most kids enjoy their time here," I replied.

"He didn't say a thing about what went on." There was an uncertain note in Lydia's voice.

"They never do," I replied, taking my seat and opening my file to my interview with Dewey. "Let me read you my notes about our interview."

I do so, and it comes out pretty much as I described earlier in this book. Lydia is shocked that Dewey had been so rude and challenging. Frank is surprised that he had been so communicative.

"His last words to me coming down here," Frank said, "Were 'I'll go but I'm not talking to some dumb shrink." Frank grinned apologetically. "I didn't know he knew the word."

"They all know that word these days." I turned to my summary formulation. "Let me give you my findings. What I've done to date is this. I've taken all the information I have gathered about Dewey, the story you told me, what I got from Miss Grant, what I learned from talking to Dewey myself, and I've pulled it together and formulated an understanding of him. It is that understanding I'd like to give you now. Today it's my turn to talk."

The sooner one gets into this the better. It is not an easy thing for parents, this coming back for the answer. They have a lot of unhappy questions in mind. How sick is he? How big a mess have we made of things? Is it too late to straighten him out? I know the questions, so I don't need to wait for them to be asked.

Frank and Lydia settled back, relieved that for the time being they were not required to participate.

"Let me say right away that Dewey's problems don't stem from any deep-seated emotional conflict. He is not neurotic. Dewey's symptoms arise because he doesn't cope as well as he should for his years. I call this adaptive immaturity because his unacceptable ways would be normal if he were four or five, but for a nine year old they are just not good enough. Dewey's maturity has lagged in three important areas. Let me tell you about these one by one."

They look at each other and nod uncertainly.

"When Dewey wants something he wants it now, he just can't wait. If he's mad, he explodes. If he's disappointed, he cries. If he has something tedious to do, he drifts from the task. The first area in which Dewey's development has lagged is with respect to patience, persistence and self-control. I call this developing tolerance for life's normal unpleasures. Dewey hasn't developed much. "

I try to tie my explanations to behaviors. There is nothing worse for parents than high-sounding explanations they cannot follow.

"Let me describe how this particular aspect of adaptive growth usually proceeds. Nobody expects a baby to wait. When you bring a baby home from the hospital you don't say to him, 'Now listen Charlie, here's the way we do things around here. After supper we go to bed and that's it until breakfast, which is seven-thirty."

They smiled.

"What you do is get up and feed him at two am, as every other parent does. We don't expect babies to wait."

"But we expect toddlers to. Not a whole lot maybe, but a bit. As the child grows we expect him or her to tolerate a little unpleasure, to wait a little. Measured doses of such minimal waiting stretch the child's capacity for unpleasure. It's a little bit like weight lifting, four pounds today, five pounds next week and in a month yesterday's challenges have become today's cinch."

Frank nodded. It was an image he could relate to.

"Dewey has lagged in this respect. He's intolerant of even minor degrees of unpleasure. The first hint of trouble with school work and he quits. If he can't find the shoe when he's dressing he gives up and grinds to a halt. This is why, unless you nag or stand over him, tedious tasks just don't get done."

"I'll say they don't," Frank said.

Lydia nodded.

"There are other kinds of unpleasure besides tedium. There's anxiety, anger, disappointment. Dewey handles all of these unpleasures poorly. Take anxiety, for example. Sure he wants to turn out for baseball, but when try-out time draws near, he starts wondering if he will drop the ball. Suddenly he loses interest. Though he won't admit it, he's afraid. He deals with this anxiety by finding a way to avoid it."

"We should have just made him go," Frank said.

"But he was **really** worried," Lydia said.

I nodded. "So are many boys, but most of them tough it out. They get the ability to little copings. Dewey's managed to avoid coping with little anxieties so he's developed less tolerance for anxiety than he needs to cope with normal childhood apprehensions."

"He can't handle disappointment either. Though he's nine he still cries when things don't work out. The same with anger. When Dewey's mad he ought to just grumble or complain. He's too old to be throwing tantrums."

I summarized, "Dewey is impatient and impulsive, he lacks persistence and self-control, and all of these qualities are manifestations of the first area of adaptive weakness, his intolerance for normal degrees of unpleasure."

"That's exactly the way he is" Frank said, "but why did he stay that way? Why didn't he grow like he should?"

"If I may, I'd like to come back to the 'how' and 'why' a little later. Dewey has three adaptive weaknesses that underlie his symptoms, and I want to tell you about all three before we ask ourselves how it all came about and what we can do about it."

Frank accepted that, but , since I could see he needed something to go on with s it, I decide to give him a little about cause. "For now, let me say just two things. Dewey has not suffered from a lack of love or nurturance. Oh, I know, you don't feel very loving towards him at times, that you've said things you've regretted, maybe over-punished too, but those troubles arise from Dewey's problems, they do not cause them. Furthermore, if you are ever going to feel more loving towards Dewey, he's first going to have to become a whole lot more lovable."

Lydia was began to relax a little.

"The second thing I'd like to say," I continued, "is that it's discipline, setting limits and expecting things of children, that stretches their tolerance for tedium. Your discipline hasn't worked as well as it should. It needs to be done again and better. The 'how' of that is what we are going to have to come back to, after I've finished telling you the other ways in which I see Dewey."

I noted, as is always the case, how attentive they were. Parents really want to understand the problem.

"The second area of adaptive delay is Dewey's self-centered way. Dewey sees the world as if he were the sun and everybody else a planet in orbit about him."

"I'll say," Frank muttered.

"Family life has to revolve around him," I continued. "He doesn't realize that others have things they want to do, at least until they make a large noise. Which most mothers are not inclined to do. 'Oh! I didn't really care about watching that show,' Mother will say as she lets him change the channel. "

Lydia smiled ruefully.

"But kids won't defer to Dewey in the way that Mother will. If he expects them to fit the play around him, they'll tell him to bug off. First thing you know he's playing with the little kids or the other rejects."

Frank nodded.

"The core problem here is that Dewey is still as self-centered as the three year old who thinks daytime starts the moment he opens his eyes in the morning."

"Three years old!"Lydia echoes softly.

"All three year olds are normally self-centered. " I continue. "So long as parents will go on accommodating to them, they'll stay that way. It's setting limits and expecting things that intrudes on normal egocentricity."

"We just wanted to make sure he was happy, but I guess we overshot a little," Frank said.

"It's natural for parents to put themselves second. After all, that's where you start from with the baby. But there comes a time when parents must begin to expect him to accommodate a little. It helps if a second child comes along."

"Another child!" Lydia said. "Just trying to cope with Dewey took all my time and attention." I

"If you had had a second child, you wouldn't have been able to accommodate as much as you did. Dewey wouldn't have liked it but it would have been good for him."

Lydia nodded uncertainly. I suspect she was wondering whether I was going to recommend she go out and get pregnant.

"But that was then, and this is now," I said. "The third adaptive delay I want to talk about has to do with accepting authority. Dewey has not made his peace with authority. It isn't just that he minds being made to do things he doesn't enjoy, all kids complain about that. No! Dewey is offended by your assuming the prerogative of requiring things of him. He doesn't concede you the right. 'You're not the boss of me' is the thought that passes through his mind."

"Comes out of his mouth," Frank corrected. "If I've heard that phrase once I've heard it a dozen times." '

"We didn't want to come on strong," Lydia said. "We tried to ask instead of tell."

"But if you ask," Frank interjected, "he just says no, and then you have to tell."

"And then he starts talking as though we were the meanest parents on the block," Lydia added. " 'Johnny doesn't have to take out the garbage. Sean doesn't have to check in right after school.' "

"It isn't taking out the garbage or coming home that offends Dewey," I said. "He sees you as bossing him about. That's why he always has to wrest some tiny concession from the expectation."

"To prove he didn't do as we ordered him to," Frank crowed. "That we aren't the boss of him. That's what I said it was."

I nodded. "And you were right. It upsets Dewey to encounter limitations on his power. He's still defending his omnipotence illusion."

"His what?" Frank asked.

"Let me explain. Babies have no idea of their powerless situati-ton. When they holler and the bottle comes, they believe their hollering made it come. The believe the world is under their control. It's an illusion that preserves their security. If they really understood their helplessness, they'd be flooded with anxiety every time the mother left the room. "

"It makes him secure, ' Lydia said, "knowing mother will come when he calls."

"That's right. That's where all children start; believing their mother is on a string and they can jerk the string," I explained. "Mothers goes along with this. They come when he calls, fetch when he says fetch. At least until he gets on his feet. Then, if Mother doesn't want to become his slave, she's going to have to deny his authority now and again."

"Or be his slave," Lydia echoed from the plains of despair.

"That's when battles-of-wills start. When Mother won't do what he says, he gets a taste of his true helplessness, his realistic dependency. He gets anxious. We call it separation anxiety."

"Separation anxiety?" Lydia queried.

I nodded. "If she's not under his control, it occurs to him she she could leave."

"Oh," Lydia said. "I see."

"So what does he do? He sets out to prove she must do as he says. He throws his spoon to the floor and orders Mother to pick it up. If Mother obeys, he wins the battle-of-wills and his omnipotence illusion is sustained; at least until the next battle."

They were nodding so I continued. "But if Mother doesn't obey, he gets a dose of his truly powerless state. 'If she doesn't have to do what I say, I could starve. She could even leave. What if she left? Where is she? Get her in here this minute.' "

"Especially at bed time?" Lydia asked.

"That's right. It's called the terrible two's. Battles of will, temper tantrums and night time settling problems all come along together."

"Then the separation anxiety is normal?" Lydia asked.

"That's right," I replied, "and it makes him fight harder to prove his omnipotence."

"Then it's a no-win situation!" Lydia exclaimed.

"Not really," I said. "Suppose he doesn't win the battle-of-wills? He fears separation, but what happens? Mother returns. His fears prove groundless. His needs are still met. Maybe not the moment he wants them to be, but they are met."

Lydia settles back in her chair.

"Slowly he begins to appreciate his situation differently. A new solution to his problem occurs. Perhaps I am not omnipotent, but perhaps I don't have to be. *Maybe I'm not the king but I'm a close friend of the king and I'm going to be all right.* So it is that children begin to trust."

"So by losing he really wins," Frank said thoughtfully.

"Exactly! Children need to lose a few battles-of-wills in order to grow adaptively. Some children don't lose any. When this happens they get hung up in the omnipotence-devaluation phase."

"Like Dewey," Frank said.

"Right. Dewey's really hung up on authority. It isn't the task that distresses him, it's Mom and Dad and Miss Grant, assuming the right to make rules. Bossing me? No way! That's why it's so important for Dewey to maintain a façade of winning."

I could see my explanation was coming together for Frank and Lydia.

"Let me just summarize a little. These are the three adaptive weaknesses behind Dewey's symptoms. He lacks tolerance for life's normal unpleasures. He has remained egocentric. He is mindlessly willful as he struggles to maintain his illusion of omnipotence."

"You got him," Frank commented.

"There's one other characteristic I need to discuss. Dewey lacks self-esteem."

"I thought that was the whole problem." Lydia said. I think she was relieved to have me broach the subject.

"Though omnipotent children like Dewey sound arrogant," I explained, "they almost always have a poor sense of worth.

"We try not to put him down," Lydia said. "It's just that he seems to expect to be perfect at things he's never done."

"He's always comparing himself to adults." Frank added.

"If you're omnipotent, you have to be as good as everybody, including adults."

"If he could accept being a child, he'd feel better about himself?" Lydia asked softly.

I nodded. "Some. But there's this too. Every time Dewey has a temper tantrum, in his heart, he knows his behavior is infantile. Every time he succeeds in avoiding some life task that other kids cope with, the price he pays is to feel weak, second rate. Self-esteem is built from coping, and since Dewey hasn't coped much he hasn't built much self-esteem."

"That's Dewey," Frank said. "The whole schmear. But what are we going to do about it?"

"We're going to have to take him through the adaptive growth he missed first time around."

"I thought loving him would be enough," Lydia said a little sadly. "But I can see it hasn't been."

"Loving a child is only half the job. It's saying 'no' and 'you must' that stretches the child's tolerance for tedium and intrudes upon his egocentricity."

"What I can't understand," Frank said, "is why we didn't manage things better the first time round. We don't think kids should make the rules. There have been plenty of storms in our house."

"I know you tried hard to discipline Dewey," I replied. "And I know there's nothing wrong with your parenting values. It's your techniques that need a little work."

"I guess we weren't too bright when it comes to being parents," Frank said.

"The first thing you did wrong, was pick the worst time to become parents. Never was there so much uncertainty about the job description. One women's magazine tells you to do this, another tells you if you do, the kid will need ten years of psychoanalyis when he grows up. There's a hundred child rearing books, ninety-two of them declaring love is all it takes, five blaming sugar, one food colouring, two still putting it all on Oedipus, one dabbling in the zodiac, another witchcraft, and a couple implicating aliens and the Chernobyl fall out. It's gotten so people don't know what parents are supposed to do anymore."

"Amen to that," Frank said.

"Another thing," I said. "With Dewey it was first time around for you and child rearing. You know what some people say: the first child, like the first waffle, should be thrown away."

Frank laughed."Or put up for adoption."

"Frank!" Lydia exclaimed.

Frank laughed. "Not really, but there have been times."

"The point I'm trying to make here is that you learn on first children. With first kids is to over-parent, to worry too much."

"I was a bit that way," Lydia confessed.

"Did you carry a mirror in your apron pocket?"

"A mirror. What for?"

"To hold by his mouth to see if he's still breathing at night."

"Do some women actually do that?" Lydia asked.

"Why do you suppose I ask the mirror question."

"Wow!" Frank said.

"Second point," I continued. "Some children are placid little creatures. If they don't what they want they wail a little, then turn their attention elsewhere. Some, like Dewey, are energetic and in-tense. When they feel even a little distress they let you know loud and clear. Put together a mother a little too anxious to do right by her child and a demanding little fire ball and it's not hard to get into some developmental trouble." I could see by Lydia's face that I'd hit pay dirt, so I carried on

"It's easy to slip into ineffective over-control."

"Ineffective over-control?" Frank echoed.

"That's shrink talk for nagging. It's over-control because you have to stand right there, 'Come on Dewey, put on your socks, find your shoes.'"

"I know that scenario," Lydia sighed. "Unless I stay right beside him the job doesn't get done."

"But next time that routine comes up, does he do any better?" Lydia shook her head.

"That's what makes it ineffective. Over-control doesn't train."

"I see," Frank said. "It's over-control because you're right there on his case, and it's ineffective because it doesn't train."

"Exactly! As you stand there supervising, it's your patience that is being exercised, not his, it's you doing the accommodating, not him."

"But how are we supposed to manage things then?" Frank asked. "If we don't stand over him, he won't do it."

When parents ask this question, I know they are past agonizing about their failure as parents, and ready to move into treatment planning.

"What we do is set up a comprehensive program to retrain him. We decide which behaviour we are going to start with and which we are going to leave alone for now. We decide how we are going to deal with the selected behavior. We divide the job between the parents. We work out detailed expectations, time limits and consequences for non-performance. I call this remedial parenting.'"

"Remedial parenting?" Lydia said. "Sort of like remedial reading, only done at home for socially illiterate kids."

" Exactly. Just a moment while I write that down for my book." And I did, and here it is.

Before I brought Lydia and Frank back for this meeting, I had blocked out the retraining program I was hoping to persuade them to set up. I have an outline I use to block out such programs. I call it my template for remedial parenting. Here it is.

Template For Remedial Parenting

[1] Select **you musts**.
      A. The bottom line program.
      B. Routines
      C. General behaviors
            Second telling
            Rude Jar
            Lie Jar
            Hit your little brother
            Etc.
      D. Specials:
            School work finishing program
            School attendance program
            Etc.

[2] Select **I wish you woulds.**
      A. For judicious neglect
      B. For the *I'll sure be glad when* approach.

[3] Make out punishment cards.

[4] Decide who does what.
      A. Father
      B. Mother
      C. Teacher

[5] Arrange for continuing supervision

Let's go through these items one at a time as I would work them out with Frank and Lydia.

Selecting the You Musts

I begin by choosing, with the parents, which areas to work on first. Obviously, if one tried to set up a program of discipline to correct everything Dewey was doing wrong, Dewey would soon be getting punished from dawn to dusk and no adaptive growth would result. There can only be a few **you musts**. Usually no more than four.

The criteria for selecting areas include the following:

I like to deal with behaviors that come up daily. The more frequent the disciplinary encounter, the faster the learning proceeds. Routines such as getting dressed in the morning or going to bed at night come up daily and so offer good opportunites to train. While these may not be the worst problems Dewey presents, they are often the easiest for parents to begin with.

With routines, expectations are naturally clear-cut, so that there can be little question of whether the job has been done or not. There can be little argument about whether Dewey is dressed, or whether he is in bed, but if the expectation was that he be polite, one can easily get into a debate over whether making faces qualifies as impolite.

It is useful if the areas for retraining are adapted to time limits, such as getting dressed and going to bed are.

However, some behaviors **must** be dealt with. If the child is stealing or refusing to go to school, one cannot ignore these symptoms and work on something easier or more convenient. There is a special instance of this which always takes priority.

A. The bottom line program

When a child is firmly required to meet a parental expectation he will usually protest. In the case of the omnipotent child this protest frequently escalates to out-of-control behavior. The grand-daddy of out-of-control behaviors is the temper tantrum. However, there are other forms of bottom line behavior such as the terminal woebegones, interminal arguing and rude defiance.

The management of temper tantrums has been dealt with at length in Chapter 4. The management of other bottom line behavior follows the same pattern. The important thing is that the child realizes that when you give him the bottom line signal, he can expect program A to follow. Here in tabular form are the steps of this program repeated.

TEMPER TANTRUM PROGRAM
The Signal
The Silent Seven
The Removal
The Timer
Persistence

Unless you have a bottom line program to use when necessary, all other programs can come to naught. This is true even of older children, except then it is a little harder to make the program work. Let me deal with the most common complication now.

Suppose, after the Silent Seven is complete, the child refuses to go to his room. What do you do? Though Father might manage to bodily remove the child, Mother won't be able to if he is really determined not to go. What is she to do?

Lean down to where he is hiding under the dining room table and tell him, "Dewey, you have one minute to go to your room. I'm not dragging you, but if you don't go, you will get a punishment card."

Mother then cuts off debate by removing herself from the scene. This is what usually happens. The first couple of times he doesn't go and gets a card. "Ha! Ha! You couldn't make me go," he declares. But did he win? At best it was a draw. Maybe he didn't go, but it did cost him.

After a couple of these, before the minute is up. he slides out from under the table and goes to his room. "Because I like it in there," he declares as stomps off. Soon he goes when he is first told to.

B Routines

Routines are the easiest behavior to program. That is why I see some omnipotent children whose routines are under quite good control despite their willfulness in other areas of family life.

Routines have another advantage. They are the one area where, with a little planning, the father can take over some of the training.

Suppose we decide to deal with two areas of routine retraining: getting dressed the morning, and going to bed at night. "Who's going to handle getting him dressed in the morning?" I ask.

If Mother is there in the morning, let her handle the dawdling over dressing. If Father is there in the evening, let him handle bedtime.

Neither is to comment on the other's performance. If Father is messing up the bedtime routine Mother should bite her tongue and retreat to the kitchen. She is off duty. And *vice versa*.

We decided Lydia will handle getting dressed in the morning and Frank will put Dewey to bed at night. Since we have handled the getting dressed routine earlier, let's talk about Father settling him at night.

Let's design our program.

PRINCIPLES OF DISCIPLINE
A clear expectancy
A time limit
Supervision if necessary
Punishment if supervise
Persist to train

The first thing we have to do is to define for the child exactly what is expected. So we agree that Dewey is to have his pajamas on and teeth brushed by a certain time. This is a timed task and either a clock or a timer ought to be involved. Father must not nag or remind but when the time is up, he is to come up to tuck Dewey in. If Dewey is not ready as prescribed, then Father is to supervise him and then tuck him in. And he gives Dewey a punishment card.

Suppose the punishment selected is that Dewey cannot ride his bike after school the next day. Father is to lock it up prior to going to work. It is not reasonable that mothers have to enforce punishments assigned by fathers.

I warned Lydia and Frank that things are liable to go differently when Father disciplines. Dewey, being a little less aware of his father's psychology than his mother's, may begin with benign compliance. "As a matter of fact, I think eight-thirty is a good time for me to go to bed; I need the sleep." And in bed he'll be. On time and everything cozy as a Walton family spelling bee.

Addressing Lydia, I completed my little story. "You can expect Frank to arrive in the kitchen and flex his child- rearing muscles for the next hour: 'You see dear, all you have to do is be firm, no pleading, no threats, just a no-nonsense statement with a smile.' "

"Bear with it," I said to Lydia. "It isn't going to last. A couple of nights of this and Dewey will start testing the limits. At first when his father arrives he will be in the middle of doing his teeth. If Father fails to punish, the next night Dewey will have his pajama top on but still have his shoes and pants to go. If Father cops out again things will get steadily worse. If Father doesn't cop out, there will be some static from Dewey, maybe an exercise of the bottom line program. After that there will be fewer claims to child rearing expertise from Father.

They both laughed.

"However," I carried on, "after three weeks of no-slip parenting you can expect Dewey to be watching the clock and rushing to get ready on time. More important of course is that he is coping with a little unpleasure, accommodating some, and accepting his father's authority."

Which is good, because each parents has to earn his own respect from the child.

What I am doing is tutoring the parents in discipline, starting out with a concrete situation, and making sure the principles of discipline are used in the design of the intervention. The goal of course is not just getting Dewey growing but also teaching the parents how to discipline effectively and eventually changing the attitudes of guilt and uncertainty which have played such a part in undermining their prior effectiveness.

C. General Behaviors

There are a number of behaviors that, coming up at various times of the day in a variety of contexts, do not so easily lend themselves to planful intervention. For example, many mothers complain of it taking six tellings and a yelling to get Dewey to move to anything, be it come for supper, come in the house, go wash his hands, and so on. For these we use the Second Telling Program detailed in a previous chapter.

I call this kind of general behavior management programs 'Jar' systems, but other methods of score-keeping besides chips in a jar can be used. One father, a billiard player, put up a biiliard score slide in the kitchen with three counters on it. One talented mother I was guiding developed a particularly effective way to score her lie program. She drew a large head of Pinocchio with a nose that could be pulled out an inch at a time. When Pinocchio's nose reached three inches, her child got a punishment and the nose returned to its normal size. How's that for non-verbal communication!

Jar programs are used with intermittent behaviors that need remediation and can serve the training agenda. I have had parents implement swear jars, hit your sister jars, lie jars, rude jars, stay-at-the-dining-room-table jars, etc. But don't line your window shelf with jars. Two at a time is plenty.

D Special Situations

If a major referral symptom was not finishing his school work, then the program outlined in Appendix B can be used. However, since this depends upon the teacher playing a part, it is not the best vehicle for turning parents into more effective disciplinarians. I would recommend it not be instituted as a beginning program. Often, as the child matures, his work performance at school tends to improve without special management.

There is another school based symptom that may need programming. If Refusal to Attend School is part of the symptom picture it needs to be dealt with promptly. The longer the child is out of school, the more difficult it becomes to get him back, and while the acute anxiety is solved by keeping the child home, adaptive growth then grinds to a halt.

This means progamming, in conjunction with the principal and teacher, a consistent method of getting him there and keeping him there.[1]

2 Select the **I Wish You Woulds**

A. Areas for Judicious Neglect

Now, having selected a few areas for programmed retraining and having assigned the task to one or another parent, we are ready to move on. I advised Frank and Lydia to let some things go. "If he has been a little rude, tell him 'that's no way to talk' and forget it. If he doesn't hang up his coat when he comes in, do it yourself and put it in the judicious neglect column. Judicious neglect is there to prevent life at home turning into a constant litany of do this, do that, punish this punish that. Leave some things alone, things like wearing matching sox, or making sure the spoon is on the same side of the place setting as the knife.

---

1   See the author's paper 'School Phobia: An Alternative Hypothesis', *Annals RCPSC*, Vol 16, No 6, Sept 1983.

B. The 'I'll sure be glad when' approach

Some mothers are quite uncomfortable with judicious neglect. "If I say nothing about something he does wrong, he'll think it's acceptable." While I feel you can always come back later and focus on some of the judicious neglect items, There is another way to deal with these. I call this the "I'll sure be glad when' approach.

You find him, make him hang up his coat, but don't punish him. Instead you say, 'I'll sure be glad when you remember to hang up your coat without being told.' Though it seems but a little thing, it has an impact.

One five-year-old-boy who was getting three areas of firm discipline and a whole lot of 'I'll sure be glad whens,' turned to his mother one day and said, "Oh! I'll sure be glad when you stop saying 'I'll sure be glad when.'"

There is a good reason for judious neglect of some items of behavior, that is to sometimes diapprove and not punish. This is an action dialogue communication. The statement it makes is one Dewys need to hear.

Dewey thinks there are two classes of people in the world: kings and slaves. This is the way omnipotent children think. They struggle against becoming a slave. One girl I saw made this very clear when she said to her mother, "You're just trying to make a slave out of me."

Her mother, who was beginning to throw off the yoke, replied, quick as a flash, "Dont be silly. If I got a slave I'd get a better one than you."

If we don't insist the omnipotent child do everything our way, we are telling him, through action dialogue, that life isn't a simple boss-or-be-bossed situation. There's something in between. This makes surrendering omnipotence illusion a more tolerable thing.

" I'm sure you are right," Lydia said, mangling her gloves some more. "But when he gives me that arrogant stare and says, 'I don't have to do what you say,' it makes me so mad I want to prove to him, then and there, who is the parent and who is the child." Just thinking about it Lydia had begun to get worked up.

What Lydia is talking about is attitude. She can't stand Dewey's nasty contempt for authority. She would like to reach in his head, turn his attitude control all the way over to 'respect your parent' and leave it there. I know how she feels. If I believed such a thing were possible, I'd transfer to neurosurgery tomorrow.

I told Lydia, " I know his attitude is hard to take, but with adaptive growth, behavior has to change before attitudes will." Lydia lookeds dubious so I spelled it out for her. "When parents are firm and don't let the child evade his responsibilities, the child learns to do what he is supposed to do and does it. That leads to behavior change. Maybe he is *rude* about it, but *he does it.*"

"When a child obeys his parent because he knows he must," I continue, "he is respecting her authority. He ignored her before, but now she makes sure he does it. Now he believes her when she says do it. In time his attitude will catch up with his behaviour.

Behaviour changes first, atttitude second. That is the only way I know of to get from this A to this B."

Because attitudes are often so offensive, parents tend to approach them head on, to either lecture the child on respecting their authority, or punish him for not doing so. At best this teaches the child to build a façade of respect. He learns to say "Yessir" and continue ignoring the chores he is supposed to do.

So behavior first, attitude second. If he is a little rude, disapprove and forget it, for now. But if he doesn't get dressed, within the time assigned, and without supervision, make it happen and give him a consequence. A month of this and you will begin to see his attitude change as well as his behavior.

"The way to retrain Dewey is to select four areas, in which to work," I said. "So far we have a temper tantrum control program, a get-dressed program, and a go-to-bed-on-time program, which Dad will run. We have room for one more, Lydia, perhaps one jar program. Which bothers you most, six telling and a yelling, or his rudeness?"

I know this is tantamount to asking her whether she would rather clean the loo or have a tooth drilled, but, whichever, it is better for it to be her choice.

She makes what I would call the right choice. But it doesn't have to be my way. "I suppose if I didn't have to tell him six times to do things, putting up with a little rude talk would be easier.'"

"OK, but make sure he hears plenty of 'I'll sure be glad when you learn not to talk rude.'"

"Oh, he will,"Lydia said grimly.

See how they toughen up when you lay it out for them?

"Now," I said, "we follow the principles of discipline: a clear expectancy, a time limit, supervision if necessary, and then a punishment because you had to supervise."

"But how can we punish when nothing bothers him?" Frank demurred.

"Let me tell you about that. That's called the sweet lemon."

3 Make out Punishment Cards

I explain to Lydia and Frank how to make and use punishment cards. Since the subject has been dealt with at length in the last chapter, I won't belabor it here.

Except for one thing. I always say, "Next week, bring your cards. We'll go over them one by one. I have learned which ones are more trouble than they are worth."

4 Decide Who Does What.

It is important to get fathers doing part of the job. Disciplining the child is one of the most loving things you can do. It is caring behavior to suffer through the least enjoyable part of parenting for your child's sake. Children need to know their fathers care too.

Also, Dewey's are liable to dismiss discipline as a strange disease with which his cranky mother is afflicted. If father helps, then he has to see discipline in a broader context, perhaps that it has something to do with the nature of life with other people.

We have already decided Lydia is going to handle the get-dressed program, Frank the go-to-bed program. If he has a temper tantrum, whoever is on the scene deals with it. Both parties are permitted to drop chips in the second telling jar, so long as they use it properly.

Obviously, Lydia is going to be doing more of this than Frank. It's a matter of logistics. Could be, with more mothers working, and fathers broadening their horizons, that will change.

It's not as big a problem as the women's magazine would ahve you think. Most mothers don't mind doing the bulk of child-rearing in the pre-school years. What turns them off is **his** doing nothing and giving **her** the *Be More Firm* lecture.

5 Arrange for Continuing Supervision

Now that we have discussed all the elements of the retraining program, what remains is for Frank and Lydia to go home and do it.

Occasionally that is all it takes. All the parents needed was someone to tell them that discipline is a legitimate part of parenting and give them a few pointers about how to do it.

When this happens it pleases me, because it means I did a good job. This result also encouraged me to write this book. If some people can make it without continuing guidance, then there must be many for whom a book that tells it straight will be all it will take. I have had a good deal of feed back confirming that this is happening.

However, the-is also makes me a little angry. Why do parents need someone to tell them it's OK to make their child mind? Who told them discipline is bad? Where did they get the idea that love is all it takes?

The books, magazines and amateur parent educators, that's who. Love is enough and discipline is bad is the message they have been promulgating for the last twenty to thirty years. No national women's magazine will publish my articles on child-rearing. They send me patronizing rejections which suggest I am out of touch with child-rearing reality.

It's still going on. I am still having to pick up the pieces of the familes and children they have harmed. Some mother and father should sue them for the damage they do with their bad advice.

Back to the matter of continuing guidance. Most parents need more than a remedial parenting program designed and communicated to them. They need continuing guidance. Usually just for a month or two.

Understanding is not always the same as doing. Many parents need someone looking over their shoulder every week for a few weeks, correcting their oversights, improving their methods, helping them understand their child's reactions to the new regimen.

What I have laid out for the Frank and Lydia is a complicated restructuring of their parenthood. Though I have tried to limit the programs to three or four areas, assigned the task and set up the punishment cards, this is a lot to remember. Implementing it can be difficult.

Sometimes there are parental habits to break.

Let me tell you a story about that. There is a delightful Irish lady of my acquaintance whose lifetime habit in any situation where conversation is possible is to begin talking, secure in the knowledge that she will soon stumble on to something to say. This had led her into some difficulty disciplining her three children.

As children will do, hers squabble in the adjoining room. When the decibels reached a certain level, Mother would go in to settle things. Well, try to settle things!

Conversationally speaking, these were certainly Mother's children. Each had an explanation for the problem. Each explanation exonerated its author and vilified the nasty siblings. Each was delivered loudly, and simultaneously.

If these parents had given their children anything in abundance, it was the freedom to speak their mind without let or hindrance.

At the same time, Mother was asking questions, not waiting for answers, and offering homilies about brotherly love and family unity. Soon enough words to fill a good-size dictionary had been uttered and nothing settled.

I designed her a special program to deal with squabbling kids. I call it the Referee Program. It has become quite popular. Here's what I told this mother to do.

The Referee Program

When the shrieking began, Mother was to call from the kitchen, "Do you want me to come and referee?" If the decibels did not settle to an acceptable level within ten seconds ,Mother was to go in and referee.

I defined refereeing as follows. "Go in. Say nothing except ,'Go to your rooms. Take no history and pay no attention to any that might be volunteered. After five minutes fetch them back. 'Now! See if you can play together without fighting.'"

Poor Mother! She tried. God how she tried. But silent refereeing was not a talent vouchsafed to her. One child, on some wildly improbable pretext, would accuse Mother of responsibility for the problem. Mother, of course, would defend herself. Another child would chime in. First thing you know it was Oxford Dictionary all over again.

"I know what I'm supposed to do," Mother said. "But I forget about calling out referee until I'm already in there and the argument's well under way."

I restressed the important elements, the called warning, the ten second interval for silence to fall, her arrival, her four word statement, the removal and the repetition.

She tried. I know she did. She's a good lady and she did her best. She got carried away, that's all.

Finally her husband found the solution. He bought her a referee's whistle, fixed it upon a wide and garish band of ribbon; the kind they use for highway dedication ceremonies. Each morning before when leaving for work he slung it around her neck and told her not to take it off until he returned home.

"That's to remind you not to go in," he explained. "Just call out Referee and wait for silence."

"That's all very well," mother said. "But if I don't get silence, what then?"

"Do what the doctor said. Go in, say you piece. And nothing more."

"They'll ask me questions. They'll make me talk. How am I going to keep from talking?"

"Stick the bloody whistle in your mouth. You can't talk with your mouth full of whistle."

"And blow it instead?"

"You don't need to blow it, " her husband explained. "The idea is to keep you from talking. Just suck on like it was a damn pacifier."

"It's working," Mother told me when she came in for her next visit. "The're squabbling, the bloody whistle is swinging around my chin, and I'm rehearsing me line. How could I forget? "You want me to come and bloody referee, " I call. A hush you could butter on bread falls on the place. The darling thing is working."

The next visit I got more details. "I've expanded a little," she said. "If one of them comes out to tell on the others, I say to him, or her, 'You want me to come and referee?' "

She laughed. "He looks at me a moment then says, 'Well now, I don't think so.' "

She laughed again. "The other day after I called out my referee bit, I sneaked over and put my ear to the door. I wanted to hear what the magic was. Here's what I heard. 'Why don't we give Carly a turn,' himself is saying. 'Then she won't fuss and Mother won't come in and referee.'"

The serious point about all this is that parents have to learn new habits. They have to train themselves if they are to retrain their children. It is my job to teach them new ways to parent. And then keep them on track while they practice the new skill.

This is child rearing consultation. It is not treatment and I wish child psychiatrists would stop calling it that. The word implies that Mother has some *neurosis* which is clouding her perception of her child and causing her to parent poorly. This is absolute nonsense.

To be sure there are neurotic mothers. Adaptively incompetent children grow up to become adults with inadequate coping styles, persons who defend against the world rather than cope with it. Some of these become mothers and they cope with parenting as poorly as they do other aspects of their adult life. Neurotic is one name for these. But they are a minority.

Most mothers I see are reasonably competent persons who have slipped into ineffective modes of parenting. While many of these women feel guilty about their parenting, this guilt is not neurotic in origin. It is situational.

These days guilt goes with motherhood like salt goes with pepper. It arises because mothers have been posed the impossible task of training the child to patience, awareness of other's rights and the acceptance of rational authority, and denied the right to discipline him. They have been besieged with the notion they must never traumatize the child by subjecting him to the pain of anxiety, disappointment or anger. At the same time, they are supposed to teach him to mind.

Bricks without straw they called such tasks in biblical times.

Since ninety percent of maternal guilt is situational, not neurotic, it does not have to be probed and analyzed. Alter the no-win situation between mother and child and the guilt melts away.

There is another reason I don't like to use the term *treatment* to refer to parent guidance. Treatment has implications, for many psychiatrists, psychologists and social workers, which distort the guidance process. For example, if the "therapist" thinks he is treating the mother, he may respond to her pleas for help in the management of her child's behavior with a remark such as, "I wonder why Pammy's throwing porridge on the walls seems to bother you so much?"

What this does is suggest to her that somehow her concern about porridge on the wall is abnormal, another manifestation of her inadequate capacity for motherhood. So is maternal guilt nurtured by therapeutic incompetence.

While such therapists says they respond to Mother's questions with questions for reasons of treatment, I suspect there is another reason, *they have no answer to offer her.* They simply don't know what to tell Mother to do about Pammy's target practice with porridge. But they are cool. They use the *I wonder* gambit. Psychiatry has a rich tradition of responding to patient questions with doctor questions, usually of the "I wonder why" type.[2]

Mothers do not need treatment, they need guidance, and the child psychiatrist undertaking this work would more properly be called a child rearing consultant than a therapist.

The Usual Course Events Take

When the parents and I meet a week later to discuss how things are going I anticipate a couple of very different responses. Some children put up horrible battles right away; others are suddenly, and surprisingly, compliant.

Dewey chose the latter course. Perhaps he detected a note of assurance in his mother's voice and, not wanting to risk his omnipotence illusion in a confrontation he might lose, he chose to comply. He "fled into health," as my dynamic colleagues would put it. If he did, at least he ran in the right direction.

"I don't understand," Lydia said. "I've been telling him that I want him up and dressed by eight and no nonsense for over a year. He paid no attention before. Suddenly I hear him saying, 'As a matter of fact, Mom, I had been planning to get an early start in the mornings for some time.' And you know he hasn't missed a morning all week."

Lydia cannot understand why Dewey suddenly obeyed. To her mind she said nothing she hadn't said a thousand times before.

The same words maybe, but they came out differently. Lydia had the get-dressed program in mind when she told Dewey to get dressed. She knew what she was going to do if he didn't, and it showed in her voice. Dewey, sensing the assurance in her voice and, not knowing what to make of it, decided to comply, at least until he figured out what was going on.

2   For a dramatic elaboration of this theme see my Leacock Nominee novel *Who's Afraid of Sigmund Freud?* , Palmer Press, Vancouver, BC.

" It won't last," I told Lydia. "His lack of persistence will let him down once his sense of urgency fades. But that's all right. You're ahead of the game. Just supervise and punish when that happens."

Parents feel that unless the child copes, progress is not being made, but I am just as content to have the child fail and be punished as to have him cope. True, when he copes his tolerance for tedium is exercised a mite, but when he doesn't make it and is punished, his omnipotence is being challneged, and that's a part of our training agenda too.

However, instant compliance is not the usual reaction to the program. Most children don't make it for three mornings in a row and have to be supervised and punished. The first two punishments the child greets with "I couldn't care less about your dumb punishment." The third day he has a tantrum, which bottom line is handled as planned.

For two, maybe three, days he makes it. Then, things having lost urgency in his mind, he slips for a day or maybe two. Then he's back on track, for four days this time.

If, on a follow-up visit, I find the program isn't working, then I review it in detail with the parents. I usually find that some principle of discipline has not been adhered to. Perhaps, instead of telling him once and coming back when his time is up, Mother, hoping to avoid having to punish him, has checked on him a couple of times. This doesn't teach him to worry about the time himself. He continues to rely upon her reminders. Indeed, the morning she doesn't, he will complain, "But you didn't remind me. You always remind me a couple of times."

Or perhaps Mother compromised on the consequence. "OK, you nearly made it. I'll accept that for today, but tomorrow be right on time or else you'll get punished. And I really mean it this time."

You can be sure tomorrow he will be even further from completion when the time is up.

This is the way parent guidance works. Through trouble-shooting, explaining and supporting, one conducts a tutorial practicum, all the time inculcating the principles of discipline and helping the parents to ventilate their concerns and clarify their prerogatives as persons. In time the parental guilt dissipates and eventually one hears some turned-the-corner phrase such as "Who's the parent around here anyway?" or "I don't know why I let that child run me, but no more."

Complications can occur and the training can get side tracked. Deweys don't give up their omnipotence without a struggle. Some demonstrate a capacity for shrewd manipulation.

One child, who chose to comply suddenly and completely, startled his mother by not only doing all the items on his morning list promptly and on time, but also adding an item. He not only washed his face, brushed his teeth and got dressed by eight, but also he made his bed, and that wasn't on the list.

For four days he did this. Then the fifth day, he didn't make his bed. His mother, confused by this gambit, told him he would be punished that night.

"That's not fair," he wailed. "Making my bed wasn't on the list. Boy, I try to be really good, and I get is punished anyway."

Poor, outsmarted mother, confused and guilty, apologized. The next morning he didn't brush his teeth, which was on the list. To make up for yesterday's unfairness, Mother didn't punish him. In three days he was back to square one, and I had a busy twenty minutes helping her understand exactly how she had been had.

As for that kid, he's so sharp one day he might even manage a job like mine.

Once one has guided the parents to reasonable success with a couple of areas of retraining, signs of adaptive growth begin to appear. There is a common pattern to such improvement.

First comes a noticeable change in the frequency and amplitude of emotional outbursts. Sometimes instead of blowing up when told to do something, he goes off grumbling.

"I can see he is making an effort to control himself," Mother reports. "He doesn't always succeed, but at least it seems to have dawned on him that he ought to try."

Next comes something like this. Mothers tell me, soft amaze-ment in their tone, "Do you know what he did? He **offered** to set the table for me! I didn't think he realized tables had to be set."

Such episodes of helpful or considerate behavior not infre-quently follow upon some particularly vociferous knock-down, drag-out exchange. It is as though the child had, for the first time, realized that his mother was truly upset with him.

I'm not convinced that he is much more mature. I think he is trying to get back in her good graces. That's OK. That's a beginning. Regardless of his motivation, for once his egocentricity has yielded to the point that he has been able to concern himself with the mental state of another than himself. A step at a time!

When he grumbles instead of defies, when he wheedles instead of insists, when he pleads instead of demands, he's beginning to surrender the omnipotence illusion.

These signs of adaptive growth are often accompanied by a change in mood, a subtle lifting of the spirit. "He seems almost happy sometimes," Mother reports. "Some of the tension seems to have gone out of him." It undoubtedly has.

However, some of this change may be in her. Most mothers are surprised and pleased to find that they can discipline effectively. Further, they are relieved to find that punishment does not make him hate her, that the next day he has gotten over his anger, indeed, seems almost more at peace with himself.

Now things start unwinding. Now that Dewey is getting dressed in the morning most of the time, Lydia is not so uptight, and mornings are no longer dreaded occasions. Lydia has stopped fussing. 'Time is running out. Is he dressing or is he dreaming? I do hope he's going to have time for some breakfast.' Now she thinks differently. 'If he's not dressing, it's his funeral. I'll supervise if I have to, but it will cost him."

Now that Dewey is making it most mornings, Lydia is pleased with him for doing it and with herself for parenting effectively. In the mornings there is time for breakfast, and since nobody's cross, the meal has become a pleasant occasion. Good will between mother and child has begun to be restored to family life. With the return of good will we can start looking forward to the day when punishment will no longer be the only effective reinforcer.

Parental guidance is the most important lever of change available to the child-rearing consultant. In my experience, when the program fails, it is usually because parental guidance fails.

Why does parental guidance sometimes fail? There are a lot of reasons.

It is not easy to face one's failures and do something about them, and despite the psychiatrist's efforts to be non-judgmental and supportive, some mothers find the process too threatening. So they slide away from the task.

Some find comfort in the notion that food additives, or perhaps sugar, are responsible for the child's tantrums. Perhaps they read an article about dyslexia and decide that their child's learning problems are to blame for eveything. Mother's opt for a diagnosis that exonertates. The big one these days is Attention Deficit Disorder.

A few decide the problem is not ineffective discipline, it is too much discipline. The buy the tale that Dewey ought to be treated as an equal not a child, that **natural consequences** is the royal road to rearing. Some of these feel parents feel they are being human and sensitive and I am inhuman and overbearing, and they depart from my office suffused with the joy of righteous indignation.

Such are a minority and by and large the results are good. Three or perhaps four months usually gets adaptive growth going to the point that only intermittent consultation is needed.

Only parents can retrain children. If parents cannot rise to the occasion, remediation fails. When this happens the omnipotent child remains omnipotent. He grows larger, but he does not grow more patient nor does he come to perceive and accommodate to the rights of others. He continues to defend his omnipotence illusion against increasing odds.

The easiest time to get adaptive growth going is first time. Sound discipline in a context of love during the pre-school years does the job. Prevention is so important that I have opted to make this the subject of another book which will be subtitled, *Promoting the Adaptive Growth of the Pre-School Child.*

The Omnipotent Adult.

The way things are, few of us achieve complete and full maturity. Many of us are still less patient than we should be, less sensitive and kind than we know we ought to be. We can all get our backs up and a little unresolved omnipotence shines through.

It is never too late to grow-up. Many mothers who have worked with me getting their Dewey on track comment at the closing. "You know, Dr Millar, I still have a bit of immaturity. I can lose my temper, I can think only of myself. I can get a bit bossy and overbearing. But you know, teaching Dewey, I've taught myself. Even my husband says I'm easier to live with . . . Now if you just work on him a bit, I think our marriage has a chance."

I always say, becoming a parent gives you another chance to grow up. God knows a whole lot of us had better do so if we are to remain top of the evolutionary tree. If we don't, and damn soon, that will be that for our species. For an opinion with respect to how far we are down that path, read Appendix C.

Appendix A

Attention Deficit Disorder

These days, unless the child is given to vegetating quietly in the corner, it is probable some physician, psychologist or teacher has labeled him Attention Deficit Disorder. What exactly does this label stand for? If he's having trouble learning it's Attention Deficit Disorder. If he's over-active or even a little distractible, it's Attention Deficit Disorder. If he has emotional or behavioral problems, these days, his chances of ending in the ADD bin are greater than Oedipus getting the blame.

ADD includes all the old labels, learning disability, hyperactivity, emotional disorder, all so fuzzed up that fifty percent of normal children can be fitted into the ADD category with little effort from the teacher who often does the labeling.

Attention Deficit Disorder is the last in a long line of labels whose primary attraction is that they relieve parental guilt. Such labels come and go. It takes a while but eventually physicians, and parents, wise up to the fact that the category is empty of meaning.

Attention Deficit Disorder has become an immensely popular label, not because it leads to effective treatment, but because, as Dr Silver, author of the CIBA pamphlet on the subject, naïvely reveals, "You may be comforted to know finally what is wrong."

The validity of a diagnosis has nothing to do with how comforting it is. But parents find the ADD label comforting. That's because it suggests the child has some mysterious something within his brain which accounts for his symptoms, and so its not their fault.

The implication is that there is something neurological not behavioral going on here. This wholly unsubstantiated notion steers treatment in exactly the wrong direction. (1)

History of the the ADD Label

Where did the label ADD come from?It evolved. Many years ago physicians noticed that children who had come from bad pregnancies or difficult births often had, in addition to their weak or spastic limbs, a tendency to be over-active and subject to what used to be called catastrophic reactions, that is explosive, out of control outbursts from minimal frustration.

Next, it was noticed there were some children who had experienced bad pregnancies and or difficult births, who showed the same behavioral actions, i.e. were over-active and had catastrophic reactions, but who did not show any spasticity or weakness.

This led to the delineation of a syndrome which was called Minimal Brain Damage. Essentially this meant there had been a degree of damage too minor to produce neurological signs and symptoms, but suff icient to disorder brain function to the point that self control became impaired.

Because there are no specific neurological signs Minimal Brain Damage is hard to diagnose. It still is. It takes a history of injury, soft neurological signs, typical over-reactive behavior, an abnormal EEG and organic signs on a psychological test. I doubt if one in fifty children diagnosed ADD has Minimal Brain Damage.

Because focal brain damage was hard to demonstrate, MBD [minimal brain damage] began to be called MBD [now meaning minimal brain dysfunction]. I don't know who authored this change, or what his evidence was, but the label caught on for a while. But soon that category fragmented in several directions at once.

Sincel symptom diagnosies such as Hyperkinesis emerged. The Etiological notions implicating sugar, food coloring, allergy, wheat germ appeared from nowhere, each with its physician promoter, each without demonstrated patho-physiology and/or proof. After some-body did a study, each cause was discredited. Another soon took its place.

Another fragment, learning difficulty also acquired the dignity of diagnostic labels, all kinds of labels, reflecting the author's notions of etiology. However, the criteria that would differentiate the truly disabled learner from the merely immature and poorly motivated child, did not survive the transition. Soon thirty percent of the children in our school were being called learning disabled.(2)

Then along came Attention Deficit Disorder, the latest entry in this field. With arrival of ADHD, this category is beginning to fragment too.

Attention Deficit Disorder posts the notion that there is some neurological based deficit in the child capacity to pay attention. Since there are no neurological or psychological test findings to indicate some lesion or abnormality in the brain is responsible, where did this idea come from? Somebody sucked it out of their thumb. They were inspired by the success of a drug, Methylphenidate, commonly known by the CIBA trade name, Ritalin.

Ritalin is a stimulant drug. Some years ago, following up on an old maid's tale about coffee, it was discovered to calm lively children. How could a stimulant drug calm children, puzzled clinicians asked. Because, some imaginative clinicians answered, it helps affected children focus their attention by stimulating their brains.

Please note, this is not knowledge, this is speculative explana-tion that adds an unproven step in the causal chain. It looks like knowledge but it isn't. There is, I am sure, no other diagnostic label in medicine that owes its origin solely to a drug effect.

The Diagnosis

ADD is not a proper medical diagnosis. It has no substantiating physical or neurological findings, no characteristic history, not even a typical clinical picture. ADD is a waste basket diagnosis.

Anyone with a pencil can make this diagnosis. All you have to do is check items on a list and add the score when you're finished. If the child exhibits eight of fourteen listed characteristics for more than six months he has ADD.

ADD is a diagnosis teachers with no medical training make every day. While, as yet, the educators are unable to presribe Ritalin, they pressure parents with threats of expulsion to get them to persuade their doctor to prescribe it.

Here are eight items from the ADD check list. In my experience many normal children, and all omnipotent children, frequently exhibit such characteristics. Could this be your child?

* Loses thing necessary for a task
* Fidgets in his seat
* Can't wait his turn
* Blurts out answers
* Shifts from one uncompleted activity to another
* Has difficulty remaining seated
* Does not listen
* Interrupts or intrudes

The fact is, Attention Deficit Disorder is a vague and over-inclusive waste-basket. It can embrace many normal children as well as immature, emotionally stressed and deprived children.

The Basics

The term ADD has a nice rhythm to it; seems to suggest precise understanding, doesn't it? All the problems of this child stem back to one root, a neurological based incapacity to maintain his attention, i. e. an attention deficit.

Let's look at this matter of attention deficit; what exactly does attention deficit mean. Does it mean the child cannot keep his attention focussed on the task at hand so he doesn't clean his room or finish his school work? Tell me this; if the job at hand is building a model, or drawing a picture of his favorite Ninja Turtle or Bart Simpson, can he keep at the task for half an hour without interruption? He can! So what kind of attention deficit are we talking about here? Better watch out Mother, because if you buy the attention deficit fairy tale you'll soon be believing him when he tells you he has DWD----Dish Washing Disability.

The child psychiatrist who labels his child patients ADD relieves parent guilt. But labels cure nothing. Now he must help Mother and Father cope with the problem behaviors. But if he tells them what they are doing wrong in their rearing, will he not resurrect the guilt? He will indeed. Having closed that door , he dare not open it again. So he fumbles along with a little play therapy for the child, a little ventilation of parental pain.

What happens now is that, after a period of no progress, the parents become dissatisfied. Now the child psychiatrist reaches for the Ritalin. And it probably will help. But this does not mean the child has ADD. Ritalin helps many lively children regardless of their diagnosis. It calms, but it does not cure.

So it is that labeling the child ADD eventually leads to Ritalin. At the same time it leads away from what these children need most, a little remedial parenting.

Many who prescribe Ritalin maintain that it is just part of an overall program of treatment that includes parental guidance. What kind of guidance? I sometimes get a chance to find out, for failed cases not infrequently arrive in my consulting room.

Here's what the parents have been hearing: "You can't expect him to keep his temper, he has an Attention Deficit Disorder. You can't expect him to finish his school work, he has Attention Deficit Disorder." What kind of retraining advice is this?

Is Ritalin Helpful?

In the short term it often is. It calms many children, and it did before ADD came on the scene. However, in the long term, there is question that the drug is useful. To cite but one study, Firestone *et al*, writing in the *American Journal of Orthopsychiatry* in 1986, concluded there was no long term benefit of stimulant medication on the behavior of the hyperactive child. (3)

What about drugging children to grow them up? Is this a good thing? In 1972 The US Food and Drug Administration and the Bureau of Narcotics pronounced Methylphenidate a dangerous drug. Sweden has simply abolished the drug as dangerous and too easy to abuse. Already there have been twenty-five published case reports of transient psychotic reactions in children which, given the sloppy medical supervision of much Ritalin use, is probably the tip of the iceberg, Furthermore the Mental Health Committee of the Canadian Pediatric Society declared that the use of Methylphenidate for ADD is potentially dangerous to the health of the child. (4)

Is There Such a Thing as ADD?

In 1987 Coles, in his book The Learning Mystique wrote about the burgeoning weakness in our diagnostic nomenclature that is countenancing loose and useless labels like ADD. I agree. ADD is not a proper diagnosis at all. What we are dealing with here is not understanding that leads to treatment. What we are dealing with here is a façade of knowledge, not knowledge itself. (5)

References

(1) Silver,L, "Attention Deficit Disorder," CIBA Pamphlet

(2) Millar, T.P. "Reading Retardation," *Northwest Medicine* November 1960, 1385-1390

(3) Firestone et al, "re efficacy of stimulants." *American Journal Orthopsychiatry*, 1986, 56: 184-19

(4) Statement of Mental Health Committee of the Canadian Pediatric Society, *Canadian Medical Association Journal*, 1990, 142:817-818

(5) Coles G,*The Learning Mystique, A Critical Look at Learning Disabilities*, Pantheon, New York 1987

(6) Kline C, Letter in *Canadian Medical Association Journal*, 1990 143 (3) 170-171

Appendix B

Finishing School Work

Indication

The program is being instituted because of the following considerations. The child is capable of doing the work. The child is not completing his regularly assigned work. The teacher has exhausted her remedies. Under these circumstances it is reasonable that the parents support the teacher's expectation that the child complete his work. 1

Goal

The goal of the program is the *completion* of classwork. It is assumed that, if a child of reasonable intelligence completes all his class work, he will absorb sufficient information to learn.

Initially, the quality of the work is not a prime consideration. While this is not a matter of indifference, it is felt that the first goal should be limited to completion. **Later** a dimension of quality may be added to the program.

Method

In order to modify the child's perception of his responsibility in the learning process it is necessary that he experience clear-cut expectations and predictable consequences if he fails to meet those expectations. This involves assignments, time limits for their completion, prompt detection of failure to complete, and reinforcing action consequent on that failure.

Assignments

The teacher assigns work. The child fails to do it. The teacher applies her normal reinforcer: miss the movie, stay in at recess, or remain after school. He still doesn't do the work. Now what? We institute the program.

If the parent is to offer effective support to the teacher's expectations, she needs to know precisely what was assigned and what was not done if she is to play her part in the program. So the teacher has to accumulate this data and send it home Friday. (We are speaking here of regular seat work, not long-range assignments.)

Communication

A foolproof method of communication between teacher and parent must be set up. I use the sealed envelope method. By the time of this publication it may have been replaced by the fax machine.

The method: All the work that was not completed during the week is **sealed** in a large manila envelope and sent home Friday. If all the work has been completed a note stating this should be placed in the envelope and the envelope sent anyway.

Trusting the child to bring the envelope home is like asking the fox to guard the chickens, but since this is the principal method of communication between parent and teacher we have to try our best to make it work. Children have been known to lose such envelopes. When this happens mothers have been known to misinterpret the situation. "Wonderful," she says. "He's finished all his work this week." By the time the truth outs , at least a week later, both parent and teacher are inclined to fault the other for the communication breakdown. Meanwhile the child has learned what nobody wanted to teach him, to wit: with a little ingenuity he can work the system and continue on his effortless path through life.

However, if Mother begins the program by handing the teacher ten dated manila envelopes on day one and explains the need for regular communication even if everything has been done, this situation can be minimized. Then, if no envelope arrives and her child declares, "I guess the teacher forget to make me one," Mother should hurry to the school, himself in tow, roust out the custodian, and search her child's desk. In many cases, en route to the school, the story will change. "Oh yes! I remember now. She gave me an envelope. I musta left it in my desk."

Communication failure can sink the program, and some children can find chinks in any system. One ingenious eleven-year-old child kept coming up with a new envelope disappearing gimmick. His mother finally rose to the occasion. She arranged for a courier to pick up the envelope at three-fifteen every Friday afternoon. After five Fridays of proving she really meant business, she told him, if she had to continue using the courier, it would cost him, either that week's video movie rental, or his next ski day. Would he like to try bringing the envelope home himself? That was the end of the communication problem.

Reinforcement

Once the parents have the unfinished work, they now have to set up the expectation that he do it. Here's the best way to do that. Begin with an explanation of the program.

"It's your job to do your schoolwork. In the class! When Miss Farrell expects you to! There's no way she can teach you if you don't do your work. She has tried her best to get you to do it but by the end of the week there's a lot not done. So now your Dad and I are going to take a hand. Here's the deal. Miss Farrell is going to send the unfinished work home in a sealed envelope every Friday, and you are going to get another chance to finish the work. You are going to have another half-day school per week: starting at nine am Saturday and finishing at noon Saturday, or when the work is finished, whichever comes first."

It doesn't have to be Saturday morning if another time suits Mother best, but it should be the same time each week. A place should be arranged with a table and materials but no toys, comic books or other distractions should be available. Mother can give him a ten-minute recess if she wants to but there he is to be until the work is finished or noon arrives, which ever comes first.

The parent is cautioned not to extend the time if he hasn't finished. When noon comes, check what he's done, put it back in the envelope with a note to his teacher saying, "As you can see he didn't finish it, but he did lose his Saturday. Hang in!"

There is no way a parent can make a child do schoolwork he is determined not to do. And if you try, say by keeping him in that room all weekend, after two weekends you're bound to weaken. All you can do is what is reasonable to do, so just persist in that.

You could sit beside him for the three hours and keep him moving, but this merely exercises your persistence. It does nothing for your child's, and it is exactly what we are trying to get out of having to do, supervise him all the time.

The teacher gets the envelope back on Monday. Seeing so little done, she may become discouraged. "What's the use, he didn't do the work?" she says to herself. She has lost sight of the fact that we are more interested in training the child to do his work without supervision than we are with the actual work itself. She is reminded of the following realities:

1. He wasn't completing his work anyway, so while we still haven't yet gained anything, neither have we lost ground.

2. Not doing the work has cost him his Saturday morning and promises to do so again next week.

3. Home and school have communicated and presented a united front which serves notice to him of a new order of things.

Course of the Program

The first Saturday the child twiddles his thumbs. "You can't make me do that dumb work you know." And he whistles and sings and variously conveys the information that he is not suffering in that work area you have arranged for him.

The next week he tries to foul up the communication, but we are ready for him and the envelope gets where it is supposed to be. Again he refuses to work. Some will try bargaining: "Tell you what. You let me watch cartoons this morning and I guarantee to do the work Sunday night." The right answer, of course, is "No way, Jose!"

To this he will probably reply, "OK then, I won't do the work." And he won't. Even so, when the time's up, let him go. Pack up the unfinished work and send it back to school Monday.

The third Saturday one of two things happens. He may throw a royal tantrum including this type of monologue: "Boy! Who do you think you are trying to make a slave out of me? It's dumb work. I'm not doing it. As soon as I'm sixteen I'm dropping out of school," etc.

Unless breakage is involved, go away and ignore.

The other thing he may do is dash off the work Friday night and say, "Ha! Ha! You can't give me your dumb old extra half day school. I've already done the work. Ha! Ha!"

There are a couple of ways to handle this. You might say "Oh phooey" and look as if he's ruined your fun with his improvement. Or you might say, "Fine. Enjoy your cartoons. But I've got an even better idea. Do your work during the week, and you won't have to do it Friday night."

The fourth week there is half as much unfinished work in the envelope.

What has happened? Some variant of this. When he gets stuck on a piece of seat work during class and is about to quit on it, he thinks, "Migawd! I'll see that Saturday," so he takes another run at it. Sometimes, when he is in after school with Wednesday's work in front of him, (the teacher should continue her normal reinforcers) instead of whiling the time away daydreaming, he does some of the work to lighten his Saturday load.

The important thing to note here is that the voice which now gets him moving is not his teacher's, or his mother's, it's his own. He is beginning to build an inner policeman with views about finishing school work. From then on he does more and more at school, either in class or afterwards, and soon there is little coming home in his Friday envelope. After eight weeks most of his work is being finished in class. Even so, the program must remain in place for at least the ten weeks for which we prepared envelopes, and longer if there's any sign of slipping.

Conclusion

The purpose of the program was to lead the child to police himself. He can think it's dumb work if he wants to, but the other kids do it and so should he.

Self-expectations begin as external expectations. If these are communicated through well-planned and consistent action-dialogue such as the program I have just described internalization of these expectations takes place. And with this comes adaptive growth.

By the time the child finishes elementary school he should have internalized his work expectations. He should feel "It is my work and I have to do it." With this attitude he is ready for the independent learning upon which success in high school depends. If he has not developed such a sense of responsibility for his work, then he is unready for high school and will sink when he gets there.

Problems and Questions

The biggest problem I encounter with this program is getting teachers to go along with it. There are a variety of reasons for this. In the first place, it puts an extra burden on them. Some are willing to go this extra mile, but some are not. Others are convinced it will not work. They have tried sending an assignment book home, usually daily, not weekly. They have seen the communication break down because the child loses the book either on the way home or on the way back.

Sometimes, by sending the book home daily, they pull Mother into nightly supervision of the child's work, which gets it done but does nothing for his work habits. Furthermore, some now complain that "Mother does all his work for him."

Another reason teachers reject the program is that it makes demands on the child. "Children should want to learn," they say. They should indeed, and some do. Those children don't need a work finishing program. However, we are talking about the sixteen to twenty-six percent of children who are not disabled and are learning poorly. Most of these children's desire to learn is not strong enough to keep them moving. Nor is their sense of obligation to the task.

The Contract Program

There is a program many teachers prefer. It is called the contract system. This is the way it is structured. The teacher and the child sit down and decide how much work he is to do that day. A contract is drawn up and both sign it.

The trouble with the contract system is that, while it may extract agreement from the child, it does not guarantee performance. If the child ignores the contract, as many do, how then is the teacher to get him to do the work?

Why is the contract system so attractive to the educators? Because of their notion that the child should want to do his work. Many teachers will say, "So long as I make him do the work, he will never learn to make himself do it."

This is wrong thinking with regard to the problem at hand. The real question is, unless somebody makes such children do the work, will they ever learn to make themselves do it? They will not. But, as we have just seen, a well-designed program to make him do the work eventually ends with the child policing himself. Maybe some day he'll even want to do it.

Another reason teacher's are attracted to the contract system is that it allows them to rationalize reducing their expectation of the child. This often stems from their concern for the child's self-esteem. "If I lower my sights a bit;give him a lesser task at which he can succeed, I'll give him a taste of success, and that will help his damaged self-steem."

Though children who are not finishing their work usually have a self-esteem problem, the contract system aggravates rather than assists with this. In the first place, often the child does even complete the lowered expectation. Not much help there eh? And, even when he does complete the work, his self-esteem is often **not** served. Let me give you an example from my practice.

A child told me about his contract. "I don't have to do the regular amount of work. Each morning Miss Gillis and I write down how much I agree to do that day."

"Agree?"

"Yep! I have to sign my name and everything."

"How much do you usually agree to do?"

"Not much," he replied, giving me a sidelong look.

"What if you don't finish? Do you have to stay after?

"Nope. Miss Gillis doesn't believe in detentions."

"What does she do then?"

"She spazzes a little then tells me to take it home and do it. But next day she mostly forgets to ask for it."

"Tell me, are you the only kid in the class on a contract?"

"Nope! Ryan's on one. He's dumb too."

'He's dumb too!' Where's the self-esteem in that statement?

Sometimes teachers object to sending the envelope weekly. It's too infrequent they say. He'll get way behind. But he's already way behind. The program did not create that situation, but it can correct it, in time.

Teachers do not always appreciate that the goal of adaptive maturational programs is not to control the behavior, it is to to train the child out of it. Too little supervision does not alter the behavior; too much does not train. By using a weekly envelope we leave room for the child to improve.

Most teachers are not so defensive that they cannot change their tune when they see things are beginning to work. But some are. For others the program is just too much work. Without the teacher's whole hearted cooperation the program will not work. When teachers are not prepared to extend themselves for the child, I cannot design a program that will work.

The same is true of parents. If they are too lazy, or too disorganized, or too soft hearted to stick to their guns, the program will fail. When parents are not prepared to extend themselves for their child, I cannot design a program that will work either.

Appendix C

Son of Big Chilly

The reason there is so much violent behavior among children and youth these days is more simple than the media would have you believe. The fact is modern parents are doing a rotten job rearing children. They have failed to lead them to normal restraint, consideration for others and the acceptance of normal authority.

Not that they meant to do so. There were just too many smarmy magazine editors telling them love is all it takes to rear children.

Modern parents have come to believe childhood should be constantly pleasurable, never boring or tedious. They tried hard to make it this way for their children. As a consequence, the children developed no patience nor persistence. They developed no tolerance for even minor unpleasure and now, when that unpleasure is anger, they let it all hang out with baseball bats and switch blades.

By constantly catering to their desires, as the child rearing books have advised, parents have allowed children to remain so egocentric they believe that, when they close their eyes, it's night for the rest of the world. Of course they do not perceive the victim at the end of their switch blade. All they are tuned to is their own trivial frustration.

By failing to discipline, parents have allowed children to retain their infantile illusion of omnipotence such that they see all authority as an unreasonable attack on their right to be wholly self determining. When they thumb their noses at the institutions of society, they truly believe they are striking a blow for freedom.

Why have modern parents done such a bad job? Are lots of them still doing it? Is there some way they can learn to do better?

The why of modern parenting goes back a way, but since it's crucial that we understand where all this came from, we have to examine those beginnings.

Most parents believe they approach their child rearing task from a base of reasoning and foresight. But parents are young people and they don't have much experience of life and growth. They do what seems right to them not realizing they are reflecting their inner selves not an understanding of the rearing process. It has always been thus.

You'd think my parents, appalled by the slaughter of World War 1 and scared witless by the Great Depression, would teach pacifism and thrift. They didn't. They reacted to their desperation by doing their boozy, flapper thing. They let us patched-pants kids grow up willy nilly. Some of us coped, some of us didn't.

You'd think my generation, pained by our careless childhoods and seared in the crucible of World War II, would turn into self as our parents did. But we didn't.

Perhaps, remembering our own childhood pain, we wanted better for our children. Well, we gave them better. Led by Freud and Spock, we spoiled our kids. We put braces on their teeth and no limits on their behaviour. We cherished their creativity and neglected to civilize them. We turned out the "now" generation, the "me" generation and the "you're not the boss of me gang." These, the Big Chillies, also known as baby boomers, rewarded us with the sexual revolution, AIDS and Yuppie consumerism.

Now the Big Chillies have reared their children. What kind of creatures have they produced? Have not their children expanded the horizons of the sexual revolution to include elementary school sex and date rape? While their parents were content to occupy the dean's office and smoke his cigars, today's children have principals cowering in the cloakroom and have takenover the halls as well as the playground. They terrorize the community and when they are apprehended, plead unhappy childhoods to youth workers as naïve as themselves. They are not impressed with societal authority either.

they can do twenty hours of community service standing on their heads.

If we would understand how the Big Chillies managed this we shall have to take a hard look at the way they approached their child rearing responsibilities. Remember, the Big Chillies were *ne pas ultra* individualists. No way was any suit-jacketed society going to interfere with their expressing every impulse in their existential repertoire. However, when they became parents, they discovered that doing their thing and meeting their child's needs tended to interfere with one another. They sought a way out. They found one. They demanded society do the job for them and **day care** became big in the land.

The Big Chillies were anti-authoritarian to the core. But disciplining children is as important a part of parenting as loving them. If you don't discipline, the terrible twos soon become the terrible threes and on to the terrible whatevers. The longer you wait, the louder the protests become, and the madder you get. The Big Chilly parents, reluctant to impose their will on innocent and free spirits, waited. And waited. Until they got mad. Suddenly **child abuse** became big in the land.

In the meantime, the schools were turning from the **pain of instruction** to their new Jerusalem, **happiness in the halls.** The result was more pandering to children, falling achievement and increasing parental distress. The solution? Sweep it under the rug. Call every thing **Learning Disability** or **Attention Deficit Disorder**, and stop issuing report cards.

This is where we are now. Thirty percent of our children with behaviou\ral or learning difficulties, an increasingly, violent fringe group, parents turning away from parenthood and schools from instruction.

Is this the way we want to rear children? Despite the mayhem in our classrooms, for many the answer is still "yes." For example, there is much pressure in Canada to expand day care as an alternative to family rearing. Much of this is emanating from feminist sources. It is self serving behavior, as egocentric as that of the children we now deplore.

These women rationalize their self service thus; if a woman is to become all that it is in her to become, she cannot subtract five or six important years from her career to raise children. So she must turn the job over to others. Obviously such women have a vested interest in believing alternative forms of rearing, day care or serial nannies, are just as good as family rearing.

The fact is these are second class forms of rearing. To be sure, good day care may be better than a bad family, but this is still not good enough. The glaring fact is, increasing numbers of children are receiving watered down mothering which is about as nourishing to the spirit as watered down milk is to the body. We are accumulating a nurturance deficit here in Canada that, in a few years, could come to rival our national debt.

Unreared children have two strikes against them. They have not received enough love to teach them the world is a giving place, and they have not received the consistent discipline that trains. Add to that a bad education and they are heading for a lifetime in the welfare dug-out.

Each generation of parents reconstructs the society in the way in which they rear their children. This is the way values are preserved and cultural growth takes place. Not to rear the children is to destroy the society. The symptoms of societal destruction are failing families, barbaric children and chaotic values.

In my work as a child psychiatrist, I have tried but there is no way I can persuade parents to get back on the job. In fact, I can't persuade many of them that there is a serious problem out there. It seesm to me, that realization involves obligations they are not willing to face.

But if they do come back to parenting, I can tell them how to do the job, indeed have written three versions of this book to do just this. It's burgeoning sales suggest there are people out there concerned to do right by their children.

Children need a reasonable amount of one-to-one mothering in their pre-school years. And, when they turn two, they need discipline to train them. By discipline I don't mean spanking, I mean planful firmness. This comes down to reasonable expectations, communicated by reasonable actions and reinforced by reasonable consequences.

Given this kind of management, children stop having temper tantrums and begin to develop patience and self control. Given this kind of steady parental input, they begin to realize they are not the center of the family, but a member of it, and their egocentricity dissipates. In time they realize they don't need to control to be safe, and they surrender their infantile omnipotence. Now trust can develop. Now they begin to cope, It is coping that generates self esteem.

The problem is not how to do the rearing job, the problem is having the will to do it. Where that is to come from in these parlous times, I do not know.

A version of this article , with a different title, one assigned by the editor, was published in the Medical Post April 27th 1993

INDEX

Parenting Programs